PERMISSION
TO
BELIEVE

Lawrence Kelemen

Targum/Feldheim

First published 1990
Second revised edition 1990
Third revised edition 1991
ISBN 0-944070-55-8

Copyright © 1990 by Lawrence Kelemen
Developed in conjunction with Yeshivat Darche Noam

Phototypeset at Targum Press

Published by:
Targum Press Inc.
22700 W. Eleven Mile Rd.
Southfield, Mich. 48034

Distributed by:
Philipp Feldheim Inc.
200 Airport Executive Park
Spring Valley, N.Y. 10977

Distributed in Israel by:
Nof Books Ltd.
POB 23646
Jerusalem 91235

Printed in Israel

"**חיש**", דפוס וכריכה, רמלה
צילום ולוחות "**פרנק**" ירושלים

RABBI SHLOMO WOLBE
39 SOROTZKIN ST.
JERUSALEM, ISRAEL

הספר " *Permission To Believe* " נכתב בכשרון רב ובסגנון
המושך את הלב. המחבר היקר, שהוא בעצמו בעל תשובה, הציב לעצמו
מטרה לכתוב חיבור עבור העוסקים בקירוב רחוקים, לתת בידם למצוא
מהלכים אל הגישה האינטלקטואליסטית של האדם האמון על התרבות
המודרנית. המחבר הצליח במשימתו, והנני מברכו כי רבים ימצאו
על ידי ספרו את המסילה לאמונה, לתורה ולקיום מצות.

הרב שלמה וולבה   עש"ק ויגש תש"ן

This book is dedicated to
the blessed memory of our grandfathers

Samuel Greenspan

Morris Gurewitz

Louis Kelemen

Curt Plotke

Lawrence and Linda Kelemen

TABLE OF CONTENTS

ACKNOWLEDGMENTS

MANY PEOPLE GUIDED this project, and all deserve credit. None, however, should be blamed for any errors, incoherence, or weaknesses in argument or presentation.

I cannot adequately express my gratitude to my parents—Henry and Dolores Kelemen—and my wife's parents—G. Jerry and Margaret Plotke—whose openness, curiosity, and unconditional love both inspired and made possible this investigation. This book would also never have been written were it not for the staff of Yeshiva University of Los Angeles in general, and Rabbis Sholom Tendler, Yitzchak Adlerstein, Nachum Sauer, and Zvi Teichman in particular. Rabbis Yisroel Herczeg, Yitzchak Hirshfeld, Yosef Kamenetzky, Shaya Karlinsky and Yitzchak Shurin, and Michael Cohen and the rest of the staff of Darche Noam/David Shapell College of Jewish Studies provided valuable insights and practical assistance. Special thanks go to Jonathan Bressel, Dr.

Ellen Bressel, Dr. Susan Gardin, Bernie and Judy Katz, Debbie Katz, Edith Reisner Newton, and Dennis Prager, all of whom graciously gave of their wisdom and editorial expertise. Dr. Leo Levi was especially helpful in editing the material relating to cosmology and teleology.

I owe two final thanks: to my wife, Linda—my beloved partner in all endeavors—whose enthusiasm, clarity, and passion for truth vitalized this project; and to God for blessing me with the family, teachers, health, peace of mind, and time that were so essential in writing this book.

Lawrence Kelemen
February, 1990
Jerusalem

INTRODUCTION

ALTHOUGH THE PURPOSE of this book is to present a rational case for God's existence, do not read further expecting absolute *scientific* or *philosophical* proof. Such proof is mathematically perfect, and requires a more thorough knowledge of our world than we possess. What follows is nothing more than permission to believe.

Also, do not read further expecting to become a believer. Some people will read this book, be unable to refute its argument, and still retain their atheism. We are complicated creatures, driven not only by the intellect, but by emotion, psyche, body, and spirit. Because we react not only to thoughts but to feelings and desires, we ultimately believe whatever we like to believe. We believe whatever makes us happy. Someone who is happy with a non-religious lifestyle, and who feels threatened by the possibility of God's existence, will be unmoved by everything that follows.

Having said all this, there are still two good reasons to argue in favor of God's existence.

First, many people would believe in God tomorrow if only their intellects would allow them. These people intuitively suspect the existence of an Almighty. Yet the admirably high value our society places on reason, combined with the unfortunately widespread misconception that belief in God is necessarily irrational, squelches their potential spirituality. These individuals should be permitted to examine the case for God. They should be granted permission to believe.

Second, many people believe in God for irrational reasons. These people have followed their intuition and made the leap of faith, and they feel compelled to leave their intellectual objections behind. They justify their faith by assuming that the intellect has no role to play in religion. The tragedy here is twofold: First, man is elevated above animals not only by his superior spirit, but by his refined mind. Barring the intellect from the religious sphere can only make the religious experience that much less sublime. Even worse, though, religion untamed by the demands of the intellect can easily go wild. Consider how many millions of innocent people have been murdered in intellectually unjustifiable religious crusades. Believers should grant their intellects permission to believe, not just to expand their religious experience, but to protect themselves from corruption.

I offer this argument, then, in the interest of truth, and in the hope that some will find here the freedom to discover God intellectually.

PERMISSION TO BELIEVE
Four Rational Approaches
to God's Existence

The first of the [Torah's] commandments is to know that there is a God.

Moses Maimonides
Sefer Hamitzvos

A person only violates a commandment when he is overcome by an irrational spirit.

Babylonian Talmud
Tractate *Sotah* 3a

CHAPTER ONE

ATHEISM IS IRRATIONAL

THERE ARE THREE possible attitudes one can have towards God: First, one can be absolutely sure that God exists. People who possess such certainty are known as believers (from the Middle English *bi-leafe*, which means "complete knowledge"). Second, one can be unsure whether there is a God. Such people are called agnostics (from the Greek *a-gignoskein*, which means "not known"). Third, one can be absolutely sure that God does not exist. These people are called atheists (from the Latin *a-theos*, which means "without God").

Only the first two of these theological attitudes are potentially sensible. The third, atheism, is necessarily irrational.

There are two ways one can be rational and believe with certainty in God. First, it is possible (at least in theory) that God might introduce Himself to you. Although we have a right to view any such claim with extreme skepticism, we must also admit that someone *could* come to possess absolute certainty about God's existence through such an event. Second, one could come to know that God exists through indirect evidence, that is, through circumstances and phenomena that cannot be explained without positing God's existence. A great deal of what we know today, we know only through such indirect evidence. For example, we know that there was once an American president by the name of Abraham Lincoln. We know this not because we ever met Lincoln, but because there is no other reasonable way to explain the existence of a universally accepted tradition that he lived. Whether direct or indirect evidence of God actually exists is a separate issue. The point here is that it is *possible* for such evidence to exist, and therefore we cannot *a priori* know that someone is irrational just because he claims to know that there is a God.

It is also possible to be rational and be uncertain if God exists, just as it is possible to be rational and be uncertain if any particular person, force, or object exists. Until one has either direct or indirect evidence, it is reasonable to remain unsure.

In contrast, it is impossible to be rational and know with certainty that God does not exist, just as it is impossible to be rational and know that *any* person, object, or force does not exist. Knowing with certainty that something does not exist requires first being aware of all things that *do* exist. This would mean simultaneously examining every cubic centimeter of the universe for the objects or forces in question. Because we cannot monitor every corner of the universe, we cannot reasonably declare the non-existence of anything—including God.

Any student of history knows how many men have made fools of themselves proclaiming the non-existence of things: of a continent west of Europe; of a particle smaller than the atom; of a natural force besides gravity and magnetism. Atheism—the state of knowing that God does not exist—is inherently irrational.

Why, then, do some very rational people claim to be atheists?

Most of them do not understand the difference between atheism and agnosticism. These people are really just healthy skeptics; lacking any evidence of God's existence, they are unwilling to call themselves believers. Once introduced to the category of agnosticism, though, these people happily re-label their attitude.

Other professed atheists understand the distinction between atheism and agnosticism but do not fully appreciate the former's inherent illogic. Most of these people were raised in non-religious homes. Since religion was a non-issue for their parents, it became a non-issue for them, and their atheism was affirmed out of inertia more than conviction. These people slip comfortably into the agnostics' camp when seriously questioned.

A smaller group of atheists affirm their atheism as a rebellion against their religious parents or school. Since most of these people rebel for emotional reasons (not intellectual ones), they are not deterred by any demonstration that their position is irrational. Their desire to condemn religion or religious people closes their minds.

The smallest group of declared atheists are highly sensitive and intelligent people. Most have never encountered arguments for God's existence, but they are woefully familiar with the single most powerful argument against it: bad things happening to good people.* Most of these people have experienced real suffering, either firsthand or through a friend or relative. For them, personal tragedy speaks only too eloquently of God's non-existence. Still, when faced with atheism's inherent irrational-

---

* This issue is dealt with in chapter six.

ity, even these people retreat to highly skeptical agnosticism.

In sum: Of the three possible attitudes one can take towards God—belief, agnosticism, and atheism—only the first two are rationally defensible. The third is a viable option only for someone who either does not know or does not care what atheism is.

And Abimelech said to Abraham, "What did you see that made you [fear for your wife Sarah]?" And Abraham said, "I said, 'There is just no awareness of God in this place, and [therefore] they will murder me to get my wife.' "

Genesis 20:10-11

CHAPTER TWO

THE MORAL APPROACH TO GOD'S EXISTENCE

MANY PEOPLE BELIEVE in universal ethics, i.e., standards of right and wrong that extend across all geographic and temporal boundaries. The popular idea that murder is always wrong—that there is something unethical about slaughtering guiltless, non-threatening human beings in any country at any period in history—is an example of just such a universal ethic.

The moral approach to God's existence begins with the question: *Why is murder wrong?* That is, who or what has the authority to establish such a universal ethical principle? Who or what *made* murder wrong?

There are many possible answers to this question.

I.

Perhaps murder is wrong because reason—abstract logic—so dictates.

The problem with such a proposal is that reason dictates that we take whatever actions will most effectively achieve our goal. Depending on our goal, reason may or may not rule out murder. If our goal is to permanently stop someone from having an effect on the world, the most effective means to that end *is* to murder that person.

There are those who might object that everyone's ultimate goal is survival, and that the most reasonable way to ensure everyone's survival is to live by and spread the ethic: refrain from doing to others what you would not want done to yourself (e.g., murder). But such an objection is doubly flawed.

First, for many people survival is not the highest value. The Japanese Kamikaze pilots who gave their lives to win World War II were not lunatics; they were highly intelligent military officers who valued Japanese victory more than their own lives. Any student of history could easily list a dozen similar examples of rational people who were willing to sacrifice themselves for the sake of abstract ideals.

Second, even those who consider their own survival their highest value might logically conclude that murdering others is a good idea. Murder, when one can get away with it and benefit in the long run, might be quite rational.

In short: Even the most perfect logic, if founded on an immoral premise, will generate an immoral conclusion. We therefore need not assume that "moral" and "rational" are equivalent. Morality and reason might be completely unrelated. Certain acts might be moral albeit irrational, and others might be immoral yet eminently reasonable. Because there is no inherent relationship between morality and logic, reason cannot be the source of the "murder is always wrong" ethic.

II.

Maybe murder is wrong because someone decided that it is.

This proposal is problematic for two reasons.

First, why should one person set the world's ethical standards? What unique trait could grant him alone the right to dictate world morality? Is it logical that the person with the highest I.Q. or the biggest army or the bluest eyes should determine absolute right and wrong? Should any human quality confer upon its possessor the status of supreme ethical authority?*

Second, what was murder's moral status before this person was born and what will it be after he dies? If someone earned the right to dictate morality by being the most unique person alive, then others must have earned this right before him and still others will do so after him. Murder's moral status would then be subject to change every eighty years or so. Thus we would not be able to affirm the premise that murder is always wrong. At best we could say that murder is wrong so long as a certain arbiter is alive. Murder can be eternally and universally unethical only if some eternal, authoritative source says so.

---

* Should one propose that the first man, being the first, had the right and authority to establish ethical principles for all his descendants, we would face the following two problems:

First, why should being first grant some sort of moral authority? Admittedly there was only one first man. But there was also only one second man, and one third man, and one millionth man. Every individual's position in history is unique. Why should being born earlier than other people endow someone with more moral authority?

Second, the archaeological record suggests that man has crafted weapons throughout his history, and anthropologists confirm that murder was in fact no less common among primitive peoples. What would lead us to believe that the first man, the progenitor of the most self-destructive species on earth, was opposed to murder?

III.

Those who would propose that murder is wrong because our society (or country) decided that it is encounter the same two problems:

There are many societies besides ours. What makes the West a moral authority over certain Eastern and African civilizations that condone infanticide, cannibalism, and other murderous behaviors? Is it logical that one group of people should dictate morality to all the others just because they speak the most articulate English or earn the highest per capita income or boast the highest geographical density of fast-food restaurants?*

Paralleling our previous objections, we must also ask what murder's moral status was before Western man condemned it and what it will be after our society's demise. Ostensibly the crown of moral arbiter was bequeathed to our society by earlier civilizations, and will in turn be passed on to some future society. Again we cannot affirm the premise that murder is *always* wrong. If murder were wrong only because our society said so, then we could at best affirm that murder has been wrong and will be wrong as long as our society survives. But murder can only be eternally and universally unethical if some source older and more authoritative than a society says so.

IV.

Maybe a federation of humanity established the eternal, universal moral principles that no person or society can.

---

* And should one suggest that the kindest (most moral) country should be appointed the world ethical authority, whose values would determine which country is the kindest? It is obviously tautological to say that the most moral country should establish what is and is not moral behavior.

Maybe murder is always wrong because the majority of mankind decided so.

This suggestion eliminates the first problem we've encountered (deciding which of many *coexisting* individuals or societies should rule). Since there is only one group which includes all mankind, that group is clearly the ultimate human authority. This suggestion does not, however, solve the second problem (deciding which of many *sequentially* existing people or societies should rule). While there is only one humanity, the members of that group keep changing. Every time someone is born, or someone dies, humanity changes. Which era, therefore, has the right to establish the ethical principles for all subsequent generations? What gives the people of 500 B.C.E. or 1500 B.C.E. more moral authority than the people of 500 C.E. or 1500 C.E.? Which humanity is the more logical heir to the moral throne?

Ultimately we must admit that murder cannot *always* be wrong just because a particular generation said so. Once again, we need a more authoritative source for eternal ethics.

The suggestion that murder is wrong because mankind said so generates a practical objection as well. During certain periods of history, the majority of mankind did not seem especially opposed to murder. After all, early man is believed to have spent much of his time either killing people or evading those who sought to kill him.

Even without speculating about prehistoric human values, we can demonstrate that modern man occasionally sanctions murder. Adolf Hitler attempted to murder every Jew in Europe, and he encountered the military opposition of fewer than twenty of the world's approximately one-hundred nations. Moreover, given that not a single unthreatened country declared war against Hitler, we can even wonder whether the handful of countries that did were motivated by a moral opposition to murder or by a survival instinct.[*]

One might argue that countries were afraid to challenge Hitler because he commanded the most aggressive army on earth, but that—in its heart—humanity opposed his genocidal campaign. But if most countries disapproved of murdering innocent Jews, then after the war—after Germany's defeat and Hitler's death—they should have enthusiastically condemned the Nazis. Yet, in 1946, when England, France, the United States, and the U.S.S.R. sought global support for the establishment of an international court to condemn war crimes and try war criminals, only nineteen countries responded.[**] If the world kept silent during the war years only out of fear, then why—*when humanity finally had a safe opportunity to declare its disapproval*—were only about a fifth of the world's nations interested?

History suggests that most of humanity did not care what Hitler did, as long as he did it to someone else. Every day of the war, for half a decade, the world reaffirmed its apathy towards Hitler and genocide.[***] And when the war was over,

---

[*] Notably, even the United States involved itself only after being attacked at Pearl Harbor, and Great Britain declared war only after Hitler publicly identified England as his next target.

[**] Greece, Denmark, Yugoslavia, the Netherlands, Czechoslovakia, Poland, Belgium, Ethiopia, Australia, Honduras, Norway, Panama, Luxembourg, Haiti, New Zealand, India, Venezuela, Uruguay, and Paraguay.

[***] Contrary to naive claims that people were silent only because they did not know what Hitler was doing, the government documents and newspaper clippings assembled since 1945 suggest that knowledge of the Holocaust was widespread even during the war. For example, on July 29, 1942, the *New York Times* reported that "Nazi authorities in Poland are planning to 'exterminate' the entire Warsaw ghetto, whose population is estimated at 600,000 Jews...." For a detailed survey of this literature, see Martin Gilbert's *Auschwitz and the Allies* (London: Arrow Books Limited, 1984).

80 percent of the world's nations declared their indifference by refusing to participate in the Nuremberg trials. If murder was wrong between 1939 and 1946, it was not because humanity *made* it wrong. Most of humanity did not care.

Thus, for philosophical as well as practical reasons, humanity cannot be the source of our ethic that murder is always wrong.

V.

Maybe murder is wrong because it is unnatural.

Immediately, we reencounter the question of when in history the ultimate moral principles were established. Nature is always changing, since individual fungi, bacteria, plants, and animals are constantly passing in and out of existence. The natural world we might have consulted a thousand years ago differs radically from our natural world. What gives prehistoric creatures more moral authority than those alive today, or vice versa? Again, any polling date we propose is necessarily arbitrary.

Moreover, even if the coalition of all living things has always agreed on basic ethical principles, that coalition might fall apart tomorrow. At best we could affirm only that a behavior has been historically considered good or evil. What that behavior's moral status will be in the future remains undecided. If we still wish to affirm the premise that murder is eternally wrong, we need a more stable source than nature.

The suggestion that murder is wrong because nature said so also generates a practical objection. If, at any point in history, we polled all living things (again, by watching their behavior), they would almost unanimously be in favor of murder. In nature, life has always been a matter of survival of the fittest, kill or be killed. Lions survive by eating innocent deer (and innocent lions, too, when the deer supply runs short). Weeds survive by strangling other plants and taking over their food supply. Bacteria, fungi, viruses, and their comrades follow similar strategies. Were we to learn any lesson from living things, it would be that murder is acceptable, if not recommended, behavior. And inanimate objects and forces are no kinder. Landslides, tidal waves, earthquakes, and lightning bolts murder indiscriminately. If murder is always wrong, it cannot be because nature made it so.

If murder is always wrong, it must be because nature was overruled. If murder is always wrong, it must be because something greater than nature decided that it should be.

VI.

There is a term for that which is greater than nature: *the supernatural*. One who wishes to affirm eternal, universal ethics like "murder is always wrong" must admit the existence of a supernatural moral arbiter, a God. There is just no other source for such ethics.

This is not a conclusive proof that God exists. Some people believe that morality is an individual, virtually aesthetic preference; that there are no universal rights or wrongs; and that murder is not absolutely evil. There are also people who prefer to believe that murder is absolutely evil, but who will abandon such a position in order to preserve their agnosticism. Both groups will be unmoved by the moral approach to God's existence. There is, however, a third group—a group persuaded that murder is universally and eternally wrong, and that other absolute moral standards also exist— and for this group the moral approach to God's existence offers permission to believe.

The world is either eternal or created in time. If it is created in time, it undoubtedly has a Creator who created it in time.

Moses Maimonides
Guide for the Perplexed, 1:71

CHAPTER THREE

THE COSMOLOGICAL APPROACH TO GOD'S EXISTENCE

I.

IN 1913 A YOUNG astronomer working for Lowell Observatory in Flagstaff, Arizona, agreed to study a mysterious glow in the sky. The observatory staff suspected that the glow might be the first glimmers of a new galaxy coming into existence, and they asked Vesto Slipher to look into the matter.[1]

Slipher ascertained that the glow was a huge group of distant stars, and he looked for the telltale rotation common to all new galaxies. To his disappointment he found that the stars were not rotating at all. This seemed to be another ordinary, static galaxy. *Andromeda*, as it was named, would be catalogued and filed away with the myriad other nebulae known to man. Andromeda was nothing special, or so Slipher thought.

Later that year Slipher discovered an error in his Andromeda calculations. The group of stars was indeed moving, but it was not rotating. It was rocketing away from the Earth at about 700,000 miles per hour. A check of some other galaxies near Andromeda provided even stranger data: They were all receding from the Earth at greater than mach speed. At the encouragement of the American Astronomical Society (which gave Slipher a standing ovation for his discovery at their 1914 meeting in Evanston, Illinois), Slipher devoted the next eleven years to documenting the apparent explosion going on around the Earth. By 1925 he had identified forty-two separate galaxies that were bolting away from us. Slipher could find no explanation for the phenomenon.

II.

Meanwhile, across the world in Germany, Albert Einstein had been formulating his Theory of General Relativity. In 1916 the first drafts of the theory became available and the scientific world went wild. It appeared that Einstein had revealed the deepest secrets of the universe. His handful of equations solved some of the most profound problems then faced by physicists, chemists, and cosmologists alike.

Einstein's equations also caused a few problems—technical dilemmas, mathematical snags—but not the sort of thing of interest to newspapers or even popular science journals. Few scientists noticed the glitches, and even fewer attempted to iron them out. Most of the world simply basked in the afterglow of general relativity.

Danish mathematician Willem de Sitter was one of the

few who did detect problems in Einstein's theory. Einstein knew and liked de Sitter and had sent him an early copy of the general relativity article. Late in 1917, only a few months after de Sitter received the paper, he returned a detailed response to Einstein. De Sitter outlined the problems with Einstein's theory and proposed a radical solution: general relativity could work only if the entire universe was exploding, erupting out in all directions from a central point. For some reason Einstein never answered de Sitter's letter.

In 1922 Soviet mathematician Alexander Friedmann independently derived de Sitter's solution. If Einstein was right, Friedmann predicted, the universe must be expanding in all directions at high speed.

Because of World War I neither de Sitter (in Denmark) nor Friedmann (in the Soviet Union) knew that young Vesto Slipher (back in the United States) was identifying dozens of receding galaxies and thus strengthening the case for an exploding universe.

When the war ended, Slipher, de Sitter, and Friedmann shared their data with Einstein. Einstein strangely resisted their solution, as if—in his brilliance—he realized the theological implications of an exploding universe. He even wrote a letter to *Zeitschrift fur Physik*, a prestigious technical journal, calling Friedmann's suggestions "suspicious."[2] Friedmann eventually proved his theory, pointing out mathematical errors in Einstein's first article, and even Einstein conceded that Slipher, de Sitter, and Friedmann were probably right. Still, he was mysteriously reluctant. "I have not yet fallen in the hands of priests," he reassured one of his colleagues;[3] and in a letter to de Sitter, he wrote, "This circumstance [of an expanding universe] irritates me."[4]

III.

Einstein was irritated for good reason. Until he assembled his Theory of General Relativity, there were three perfectly acceptable descriptions of the universe:

(A) The universe might be static, an infinite splash of stars and planets sitting virtually still in space. Even according to this theory, a few stars and planets could be orbiting larger stars and planets or sliding across the dark emptiness of space. But basically, the universe would be stationary. Such a universe (called *static*) could have been created by God at some point in history, but it also could have existed forever without God.

(B) Or the universe might be a cosmic balloon alternately expanding and contracting. For a few billion years it would inflate into absolute nothingness. The gravitational attraction of every star and planet pulling on every other

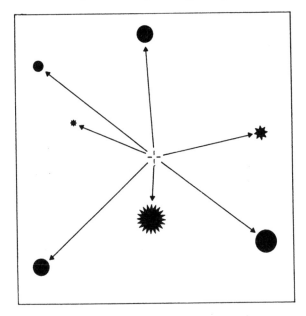

THE MOMENTUM OF THE BIG BANG
drives all stars and planets away from
the universe's center.

would eventually slow this expansion until the whole process would reverse and the balloon would come crashing back in upon itself. All that existed would eventually smash together at the universe's center, releasing huge amounts of heat and light, spewing everything back out in all directions and beginning the expansion phase all over again. This implosion-explosion cycle could go on forever. Such a universe (called *oscillating*) could also have existed forever without God.

(C) Or, finally, the universe might be a cosmic balloon that never implodes. If the total gravitational attraction of all stars and planets could not halt the initial expansion, the universe would spill out into nothingness forever. Eventually the stars would burn out and a curtain of frozen darkness

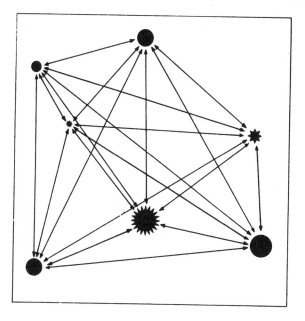

COSMOLOGISTS WONDER whether the gravitational pull of all cosmic bodies on each other might eventually slow or even reverse the universe's expansion.

would enshroud all existence. Such a universe (called *open*) could never bring itself back to life. It would come into existence at a moment in history, blaze gloriously, and then pass into irrevocable night.

The open model generates an uncomfortable question: Why would a dot containing all matter and energy—a dot that sat quietly for an eternity—suddenly explode? The Law of Inertia insists that objects at rest should remain at rest unless acted upon by an external force. Since all matter and energy would be contained within this dot, there could be nothing outside the dot to get things going—nothing natural, at least. What force could have ignited the initial explosion?

And even if one were tempted to answer that the dot was never stable—that it popped into existence in its unstable form and immediately exploded—one would still have to explain how anything could pop into existence. The Law of Conservation of Matter and Energy dictates that the total matter and energy in the universe cannot increase or decrease. How can one begin to suggest the instantaneous, *ex-nihilo* creation of the universe without slipping into a theological discourse? The third model thus seems to assume a supernatural Creator.

Until Slipher, de Sitter, and Friedmann got involved, all three models of the universe were equally plausible. Now, though, the static model was threatened. If de Sitter and Friedmann were right, then the universe was not static; it was exploding. And if the universe was exploding, then it might have been created. Einstein felt religion and science drawing uncomfortably close.

Still, Einstein realized, nothing had been proven. Slipher had only demonstrated that a few dozen galaxies were receding from the Earth. That was a far cry from proving that the whole universe was exploding. Furthermore, de Sitter and

Friedmann based their predictions of an open universe on the Theory of General Relativity; but general relativity itself had yet to be confirmed. And finally, even if the universe's expansion and general relativity could be proven, only a demonstration that the universe would never recollapse would push cosmologists to religious conclusions.

Einstein rested easy, but only briefly. In 1925, Edwin Hubble, an American astronomer working at Mount Wilson Observatory in California, dealt the static model of the universe a fatal blow. Using what was then the largest telescope in the world, Hubble revealed that every galaxy within 100 million light years* of the Earth was receding.

Einstein tenaciously refused to acknowledge Hubble's work. The German genius continued teaching the static model for five more years, until, at Hubble's request, he traveled from Berlin to Pasadena to personally examine the evidence. At the trip's conclusion, Einstein reluctantly admitted, "New observations by Hubble...make it appear likely that the general structure of the universe is not static."[5]

Einstein died in 1955, swayed but still not fully convinced that the universe was expanding.

IV.

Ten years later, in 1965, Arno Penzias and Robert Wilson were calibrating a super-sensitive microwave detector at Bell Telephone Laboratories in New Jersey. No matter where the two scientists aimed the instrument, it picked up the same unidentified background noise. At first they thought bird droppings had damaged the detector's antenna, but repeated cleanings did nothing to alleviate the noise. Then they thought a local broadcaster had accidentally jammed

---

* 6×10^{17} miles.

their receiver, but a search of the surrounding cities turned up no such microwave source. Finally they overhauled their whole electronic system, but the noise just kept coming: a steady, three-degree Kelvin ("3K") hum.

Penzias and Wilson began a serious study of the microwave noise. First they discovered that the "3K hum" was coming from outside our atmosphere, and then they found that it was coming from outside our solar system. Eventually their tests proved that the noise filled every corner of the observable universe. On a hunch, the two Bell Labs employees looked over an essay on general relativity by a student of a student of Alexander Friedmann. The essay predicted that remnants of the universe's most recent explosion should be detectable in the form of weak microwave radiation, "around 5K, or thereabouts."[6] The two scientists realized they had discovered the echo of the biggest explosion in history: "the Big Bang." For this discovery, Penzias and Wilson received the Nobel Prize.

The discovery of the "3K hum" sparked interest in another prediction based on general relativity: If there really had been a Big Bang, the super-hot temperatures in the first few moments after the explosion should have produced huge amounts of certain elements. Specifically, the universe should be made up of about 75 percent hydrogen, 25 percent helium, and one-part-in-a-million all the other elements. In the flood of Big Bang research that followed the Penzias and Wilson discovery, this prediction was also precisely confirmed.[7]

The discoveries of both the "3K hum" and the predicted balance of elements undermined the static model of the universe. There were only two models left: one worked without God and one did not. The last issue to be settled was: Had the universe exploded an infinite number of times? Or only once?

Researchers knew that the issue could be settled by determining the average density of the universe. If the universe contained the equivalent of about one hydrogen atom per ten cubic feet of space,[8] then the gravitational attraction among all the universe's particles would be strong enough to stop and reverse the expansion. Eventually there would be a "Big Crunch" which would lead to another Big Bang (and then another Big Crunch, etc.). If, on the other hand, the universe contained less than this density, then the Big Bang's explosive force would overcome all the gravitational pulls, and everything would sail out into nothingness forever.

Between 1965 and 1978, scientists attempted to determine the universe's average density. Time after time the measurements came out to be less than one hydrogen atom per ten cubic feet of space, sometimes by orders of a thousand or more.

Curiously, a sort of panic seized the scientific world. Mathematicians, physicists, astronomers, and cosmologists joined forces to prove the eternity of the universe. Some suggested that the missing matter might be spread across the universe in the form of either radiation (which Einstein proved also has weight)* or very thin, invisible gas. Others submitted that the missing matter might have taken the form of gigantic stars resting undetectably inside black holes. But study after study undermined these theories. Fifteen years of research failed to turn up any significant evidence of the missing matter.

In 1978 Dr. Robert Jastrow, director of the National Aeronautics and Space Administration's Goddard Center for Space Studies, made a historic announcement. Even after taking

---

* Once Einstein proved that E (energy) = M (mass) x C^2 (the speed of light, squared), the scientific world accepted the fact that radiation is just a very dilute form of matter. Thus, when weighing the universe, even the weight of radiation had to be taken into account.

into account radiation, gas, black holes, and other forms of invisible matter, he explained, the maximum total weight of the universe "is still more than ten times too small to bring the expansion...to a halt."[9] In an article he wrote for the *New York Times Magazine,* Jastrow declared that the third (open) model was probably correct.[10]

Dr. James Trefil, a physicist at the University of Virginia, independently confirmed Jastrow's discovery in 1983.[11] Drs. John Barrow (an astronomer at the University of Sussex) and Frank Tipler (a mathematician and physicist at Tulane University) published similar results in 1986.[12] In 1988, Dr. Stephen Hawking, a mathematician and theoretical physicist at Cambridge University, confirmed the findings of Jastrow, Trefil, Barrow, and Tipler. "Many people do not like the idea that time has a beginning, probably because it smacks of divine intervention," he writes. Nonetheless, "the present evidence suggests that the universe will probably expand forever."[13]

At the 1990 meeting of the American Astronomical Society, Professor John Mather of Columbia University, an astrophysicist who also serves on the staff of NASA's Goddard Center, presented "the most dramatic support ever" for an open universe.[14] According to a journalist present, Mather's keynote address was greeted with thunderous applause, which led the meeting's chairman, Dr. Geoffrey Burbidge, to comment: "It seems clear that the audience is in favor of the book of Genesis—at least the first verse or so, which seems to have been confirmed."[15]

V.

But what if Jastrow, Trefil, Barrow, Tipler, Hawking, Mather, and their colleagues are all wrong? What if the missing matter turns up tomorrow? Professor Stanley Jaki, of the University of Edinburgh, notes that even if we find the extra mass, thereby reviving the oscillating model of the universe:

> The process [of expansion and contraction] would not go on ad infinitum. There has not yet been found any physical process that would be exempt from the law of entropy. Indeed, more and more attention has been given recently to the rate at which subsequent cycles in an oscillating universe would be less and less energetic. It is indeed possible to calculate, however tentatively, the number of cycles which would bring us back in time to the point where the period of a cycle would be vanishingly small.[16]

In short, no process can go on forever. Even if the oscillating model were accurate and the universe exploded once or twice or a hundred times previously, sometime it will explode for the last time.[17] Which means that sometime it exploded for the first time. Again, we must explain what force brought the universe into existence and what force caused the first Big Bang. As Jastrow described in his New York Times Magazine article, the scientific world is acutely aware of its recent work's theological significance:

> This is an exceedingly strange development, unexpected by all but the theologians. They have always accepted the word of the Bible: In the beginning God created heaven and earth.... For the scientist who has lived by his faith in the power of reason, the story ends like a bad dream. He has scaled the mountains of ignorance; he is about to conquer the highest peak; as he pulls himself over the final rock, he is greeted by a band of theologians who have been sitting there for centuries.[18]

There are, of course, mathematicians, physicists, astronomers, and cosmologists who choose not to believe in God today. For a variety of reasons, they choose instead to trust that new laws will be discovered or that new evidence will appear and overturn the current model of an open, created universe. But for many in the scientific community, the evidence is persuasive. For many, modern cosmology offers permission to believe.

NOTES

1. Unless otherwise noted, the historical data in this chapter can be found in Robert Jastrow's *God and the Astronomers* (New York: Warner Books, 1984).

2. Ibid., p. 27.

3. Stanley L. Jaki, "From Scientific Cosmology to a Created Universe," in *Intellectuals Speak Out About God*, Roy A. Varghese (Chicago: Regnery Gateway Inc., 1984), p. 76.

4. Jastrow, p. 29.

5. Ibid., p. 55.

6. John D. Barrow and Frank J. Tipler, *The Anthropic Cosmological Principle* (Oxford: Clarendon Press, 1987), p. 368.

7. Ibid., p. 369.

8. Jastrow, p. 131.

9. Ibid., p. 132.

10. Jastrow, "Have Astronomers Found God?" *New York Times Magazine*, 25 June 1978.

11. James S. Trefil, *The Moment of Creation* (New York: Macmillan Publishing Company, 1983), pp. 213-214.

12. Barrow and Tipler, pp. 601-627.

13. Stephen W. Hawking, *A Brief History of Time* (New York: Bantam Books, 1988), p. 46. Also see John Horgan, "Trends in Cosmology," *Scientific American*, October 1990, pp. 78-79.

14. David Chandler, "Satellite's New Data Smoothly Supports Big Bang Theory," *Boston Sunday Globe*, 14 January 1990.

15. Ibid.

16. Jaki, p. 75.

17. Also see Heinz R. Pagels, *Perfect Symmetry: The Search for the Beginning of Time* (New York: Simon and Schuster, 1985), pp. 229-237.

18. Jastrow, "Have Astronomers Found God?" p. 29.

Rabbi Isaac said: A traveler once happened upon a castle engulfed in flames and asked himself, "Is it possible that this castle has no steward?" Just then the castle owner appeared to him and said, "I am the master of the castle." So, too, Abraham our forefather asked, "Can one say that this world has no architect and supervisor?" Just then the Holy One, blessed be He, appeared to Abraham and said, "I am the Master of the world."

Genesis Rabbah 39:1

CHAPTER FOUR

THE
TELEOLOGICAL APPROACH
TO GOD'S EXISTENCE

I.

THE INTRICATE STRUCTURE of the world has astounded man for millennia, and modern scientific advances have done nothing to attenuate that astonishment. In fact, during this century researchers have revealed aspects of the universe's structure that make all the design observations of the previous two thousand years seem insignificant.

Consider, for example, James Watson and Francis Crick's 1953 discovery of the structure and function of deoxyribonucleic acid (DNA), a chain of chemicals found in every human cell. Watson and Crick proved that DNA contains an exact blueprint of the body's every physical detail: fingerprints and toeprints; skin, hair, and eye color; heart size and shape. Everything.

DNA can be compared to a digital computer: A single bit of computer memory can hold only a zero or a one, but a computer can store whole images by translating them into a code of millions of zeroes and ones. Likewise, the rungs of the DNA helix can be only type A (adenine + thymine) or type B (cytosine + guanine), yet the DNA chain can store a comprehensive, 3-D picture of your body by translating that picture into a code of about three million type-A and type-B rungs. DNA is unlike any modern computer, though, in its storage efficiency. If stored electronically, the massive map contained in a single DNA chain would take up trillions of computer bytes. Yet DNA crams all this information into a tiny, double-helix shaped molecule equipped with the equivalent of only about 375 million computer bytes.*

DNA accomplishes this feat by storing messages in layers. Many rungs in the ladder participate in several overlapping messages simultaneously. Dr. Michael Denton, an Australian microbiologist, explains this phenomenon by comparing the genetic code to Morse code. "One sequence of symbols in Morse code can contain information for two words and be read in two different ways,"[1] he points out, illustrating with this example:

---

* Each of the three billion rungs of the DNA double-helix is capable of storing a single binary code, like the 0 or 1 stored in a single bit of computer memory. Since there are eight bits in a computer byte, DNA's three billion rungs correspond to roughly 375 million bytes of computer storage.

Letter	Morse Code
A	• —
I	• •
M	— —
N	— •

Overlapping Messages

M   A   N   A

— — • — — • • — • • •

    M   I   N   I

This one line of Morse code, with only enough dots and dashes to code about five letters, can code eight letters when two messages overlap. In theory, a code could be layered dozens or hundreds of messages deep, although computer scientists have not devised a method for accomplishing this density. Fantastically, this is just what DNA does, storing in a ladder of only a few billion rungs the designs for body parts made of trillions and trillions of cells. In Denton's words:

> The capacity of DNA to store information vastly exceeds that of any other known system; it is so efficient that all the information needed to specify an organism as complex as man weighs less than a few thousand millionths of a gram. The information necessary to specify the design of all the species of organisms which have ever existed on the planet...could be held in a teaspoon and there would still be room left for all the information in every book ever written.[2]

How does the body know where in the DNA chain to begin reading the code for, say, a nose? How does it avoid accidentally reading the wrong message and putting our ear or elbow where our nose should go? The DNA code starts with a table of contents, so to speak. One of the chain's first coded messages tells the body where to look in the chain for all the other messages. The DNA chain also contains a coded description of itself. Every time the body builds a new cell, the parent cell's DNA chain looks into itself, reads its own blueprint, and reproduces an exact copy of itself for the new cell.

The marvel of the universe's design does not end with DNA. Each body part coded into the DNA chain manifests a sophisticated structure. Our eye, for instance, contains about seven million cone-shaped color sensors, bringing us gleaming detail over a huge range of lighting conditions. Whenever there is insufficient light for accurate color vision, the cone-shaped sensors deactivate themselves and about 120 million rod-shaped, ultra-sensitive black-and-white sensors switch on. Another computer in our optic nerve accepts the signals from these 127 million sensors, recodes them into more compact signals, and shoots them down the few hundred thousand nerve fibers leading to our brain at about a billion impulses per second. And while all this is going on: the pupil is monitoring and maintaining a consistent illumination level within our eye; a stereo focusing system is adjusting focal lengths for maximum image sharpness; and a sophisticated image-enhancer is clarifying tiny blurs in our vision caused by motion and/or darkness.

Besides the two video units mounted in our head, we are equipped with equally complex devices for detecting and analyzing sounds, tastes, and smells. Virtually every square centimeter of our body is packed with pressure and temperature sensors, and balance detectors mounted on both sides of our skull constantly report our orientation to the Earth's surface. Our immune system instantly detects and responds to viral and bacterial intruders. Our respiratory and circulatory systems maintain a perfect oxygen/carbon-dioxide balance throughout the

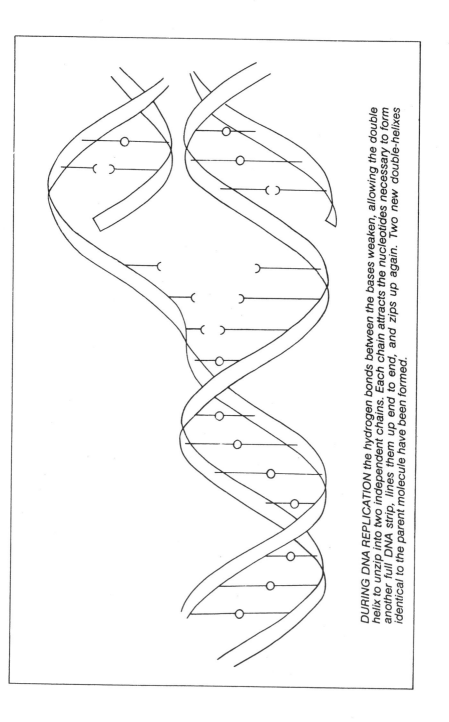

DURING DNA REPLICATION the hydrogen bonds between the bases weaken, allowing the double helix to unzip into two independent chains. Each chain attracts the nucleotides necessary to form another full DNA strip, lines them up end to end, and zips up again. Two new double-helixes identical to the parent molecule have been formed.

body. And our digestive system removes and stores valuable proteins, carbohydrates, and fats from foods, separating and excreting compounds that the body cannot use. A perfectly fit ball-in-socket system allows our bones fluid movement; tendons, ligaments, and skin bind our limbs together without compromising flexibility; and muscles drive the whole skeletal system, responding with equal precision to the subtlest and most intense neural messages. Meanwhile, at every moment, the brain and its network of more than a million billion neural connections reach out to supervise all these operations and more.

Man has never succeeded in building a computer that can match DNA's data-storage and reproductive capabilities. Neither has he ever constructed a television camera that can mimic the human eye's brightness range, focal flexibility, and image-processing abilities. Nor has he yet assembled a communications network with as many specific connections as a single human brain.* The human body dwarfs in complexity any object man has ever designed.

And thus far, we have focused only on the order obvious in human beings. We have not mentioned the immensely sophisticated designs inherent in plants, fish, birds, and other animals. Suffice it to say that the blueprints for building a fully functional tree, shark, hummingbird, scorpion, or gorilla would eclipse the plans for the United States' most sophisticated jet-fighter.

We also have not discussed the immensely sophisticated physical design of the Earth, the solar system, and other galaxies. For example, if our atmosphere lacked carbon, hy-

---

* Denton points out, "Even if only one-hundredth of the connections in the brain were specifically organized, this would still represent a system containing a much greater number of specific connections than in the entire communications network on Earth" (pp. 330-331).

drogen, oxygen, or nitrogen—or even contained all four elements, but in different proportions—life as we know it would be impossible. Were the Earth's average air temperature a mere ten degrees higher, surface rocks would release higher levels of CO_2, stimulating a runaway greenhouse effect that would boil away the oceans and destroy all life. Conversely, were the Earth's average air temperature ten degrees cooler, glacial icing would increase at the polar caps, raising the percentage of solar heat reflected back into space and setting off a lethal, global glaciation.[3] Another example: Had the primordial Earth fallen into a slightly tighter orbit around the sun, our planet would have been incinerated millions of years ago. Had the primordial Earth fallen into a slightly wider orbit around the sun, our planet would have escaped into frozen, intergalactic darkness. Consider: If the rate of the universe's expansion one second after the Big Bang had been smaller by even one part in a hundred thousand million million, the universe would have recollapsed before ever reaching its present size.[4]* Finally, it must be apparent that our daily survival depends on the amazing coincidence that none of the billions of meteorites, planets, and stars flying around our universe crashes into the Earth.

Still we have not looked at the precisely balanced laws of physics and chemistry. For example, minute changes in the strength of the electromagnetic or nuclear Strong and Weak forces would prevent the formation of biologically essential nuclei like carbon and hydrogen.[5] Slight alterations in the strength of the gravitational force would prevent the formation of planets and stars.[6] The probability that all of these natural forces would randomly settle at the precise strengths

---

* Yale University's Lawrence M. Krauss has compared the odds of the universe expanding at precisely the right rate to "the odds of someone guessing *exactly* how many atoms are in the sun" (*Scientific American*, October 1990, p. 78).

necessary to sustain a biotic environment is infinitesimal, as is the probability that these forces would maintain their perfect alignment every moment of the last thirty billion years.

The more one looks into the universe, the more precision and order he sees; and all of this precision and order—all of this design—generates a question: *Who or what designed everything?*

II.

There are two types of explanations for the universe's design: natural explanations, and supernatural explanations. Natural explanations fall into two categories: theories that posit the existence of ordering forces, and theories that propose that random, entropic forces have accidentally produced an ordered universe. To date there is no evidence of ordering forces in nature. In fact, the Second Law of Thermodynamics (known as the Law of Entropy) declares that the total order in the universe constantly decays. There is, however, evidence that, given enough time, random forces can accidentally produce order. Of the theories based on this evidence, the most developed is the theory of evolution.

Neo-Darwinian theory speculates that the ingredients of a primordial chemical soup randomly combined and recombined until viable primitive life formed. That first living thing then reproduced abundantly, as did its offspring, occasionally producing mutant species. These species also reproduced and generated new, more sophisticated mutants, ultimately yielding the range of living creatures alive today. (Interestingly, Charles Darwin never actually suggested that evolutionary forces could transform dead matter into living creatures. Rather, his theory explained only how lower life forms could evolve into more sophisticated ones. It was Darwin's students who later expanded his theory to include even the formation of the first living creature.)

When Darwin first proposed evolution in 1859, it was only a theory based on unsupported premises. To Darwin's disappointment, the essential evidence needed to transform the theory into fact did not materialize during his lifetime; nor has such evidence materialized today.*

There are essentially two lines of missing evidence. First, neo-Darwinism (which proposes the evolution of life from inanimate matter) depends on the existence of a prebiotic soup rich in all the ingredients necessary for life. Yet, to date, paleontologists have been unable to confirm that such a soup ever existed. The oldest sediments yet recovered "show no sign of any abiotically formed organic compounds."[7] Drs. J. Brooks and G. Shaw of the University of Bradford (England) School of Chemistry concluded in their 1978 report *Critical Assessment of the Origin of Life*: "There is no evidence that a 'primeval soup' ever existed on this planet for any appreciable length of time."[8] Nobel Prize-winning astronomer and chemist Dr. Fred Hoyle** and his British co-author, chemist Chandra Wickramasinghe, write in their famous *Lifecloud*: "In accepting the 'primeval soup theory' of the origin of life, scientists have replaced the religious mysteries which shrouded this question with equally mysterious scientific dogmas."[9] Thus the first premise of neo-Darwinism—that a primordial prebiotic soup once existed—remains unsubstantiated today.

----

* John Horgan, a member of *Scientific American*'s Board of Editors, wrote in 1991, "Although this scenario [of evolution] is already ensconced in textbooks, it has been seriously challenged of late" (*Scientific American*, February 1991, p. 102).

** Hoyle also served as president of England's Royal Astronomical Society, vice-president of the Royal Society, and a foreign associate of the United States National Academy of Science.

The second piece of missing evidence concerns the fossil record. If the theory of evolution were true, then every species would have been preceded by a nearly identical parent-species. In *The Origin of Species*, Darwin himself admits that such a gradually evolving series of fossils had yet to be discovered:

> Geological research, though it has added numerous species to existing and extinct genera, and has made the intervals between some few groups less wide than they otherwise would have been, yet has done scarcely anything in breaking the distinction between species, by connecting them together by numerous, fine, intermediate varieties; and this not having been affected is probably the gravest and most obvious of all the many objections which may be urged against my views.[10]

While Darwin had faith that paleontologists would one day discover the missing links, more modern research suggests that they will never be found. Professor N. Heribert-Nilsson of Lund University, Sweden, disclosed back in 1954, "The fossil material is now so complete that the lack of transitional series cannot be explained by the scarcity of the material."[11] He concludes his book *Synthetische Artbildung*: "It is not even possible to make a caricature of evolution out of palaeobiological facts....The deficiencies are real, they will never be filled."[12]

Modern scholars are acutely aware of how accurate Heribert-Nilsson's prophecy was. "Probably most people assume that fossils provide a very important part of the general argument that is made in favor of Darwinian interpretations of the history of life," writes David M. Raup, curator of Chicago's Field Museum of Natural History. "Unfortunately, this is not strictly true."[13] Raup reported in 1979:

Instead of finding the gradual unfolding of life, what geologists of Darwin's time and geologists of the present day actually find is a highly uneven or jerky record; that is, species appear in the sequence very suddenly, show little or no change during their existence in the record, then abruptly go out of the record.[14]

Microbiologist Denton wrote in 1985:

Despite the tremendous increase in geological activity in every corner of the globe and despite the discovery of many strange and hitherto unknown forms, the infinitude of connecting links has still not been discovered and the fossil record is about as discontinuous as it was when Darwin was writing the *Origin*.[15]

One can hope that the missing links will someday appear, but currently the theory of evolution's second premise also remains unproven.

More disconcerting to Darwinists than the missing evidence, however, is the existence of apparently contradictory evidence. Consider, for example: The theory of evolution teaches that new organs must evolve in tiny stages over a long period of time. Darwin himself wrote in *The Origin of Species*: "If it could be demonstrated that any complex organ existed which could not possibly have been formed by numerous, successive, slight modifications, my theory would absolutely break down."[16] Yet a myriad of such organs have been identified. Thus entomologist Robin John Tillyard, professor of zoology at the University of Sydney, remarked cryptically in 1917: "The [mating] apparatus of the male Dragonfly is not homologous with any known organ in the Animal Kingdom; it is not derived from any pre-existing organ; and its origin, therefore, is as complete a mystery as it well could be."[17]

Botanist Francis Ernest Lloyd confessed similar amazement in 1942. Regarding the origin of carnivorous plants (such as the Venus Fly Trap), he wrote: "How the highly specialized organs of capture could have evolved seems to defy our present knowledge."[18] In 1965, another botanist, Claude Wilson Wardlaw, echoed Lloyd's sentiments, writing about flora in general:

> Special adaptive features such as those exemplified by the plants of special habitats, climbing plants, insectivorous plants, the numerous cunning floral arrangements that ensure cross-pollination, and so on virtually ad libitum, seem to the writer to be difficult to account for adequately in terms of a sequence of small random variations, and natural selection.[19]

Parasitologist Asa Crawford Chandler admitted in 1961: "It would be difficult, if not impossible, to explain, step by step, the details of the process of evolution by which some of the highly specialized parasites reached their present condition."[20]

In 1974, paleontologist Barbara Stahl said about bird feathers, "How they arose initially, presumably from reptile scales, defies analysis."[21] And writing in *American Scientist*, Professor Richard B. Goldsmidt, a biologist with the University of California at Berkeley, challenged his Darwinian colleagues to explain bird feathers and sixteen other features that defy evolutionary development, including mammal hair, arthropod and vertebrate segmentation, the transformation of gill arches, teeth, mollusc shells, blood circulation, the poison mechanism of snakes, the whalebone, and compound eyes.[22] Proponents of the theory of evolution must either close their eyes to the existence of these body parts, or—again—have faith that someday the difficulties caused by such evidence will be explained away.

Theoretical problems also plague neo-Darwinism. For example, most researchers now believe that a prebiotic soup could never have existed. Such a soup, they point out, would require an oxygen-free environment, since oxygen would react with and destroy the mixture's essential chemicals. But an environment without oxygen (and thus without ozone)[*] would leave the Earth's surface unshielded from the sun's deadly ultraviolet radiation. Therefore, any life that managed to form would be instantly and mortally irradiated.[23] Moreover, such a soup would need to contain many complex organic compounds. But studies show that such compounds are unstable, tending to quickly redissolve into solution. The soup simply would not last long enough to breed any really promising molecules.[24]

Another theoretical flaw grew out of Darwin's incomplete understanding of genetics. Darwin assumed that any species could slowly evolve into any other species through a series of small changes. But scientists now know that genes have mutability limits. A DNA chain will stretch only so far from its original form before breaking or snapping back. This principle was first identified in 1948 by Harvard University geneticist Ernst Mayr. He deduced this theory, which he called "genetic homeostasis," from tests performed on the *Drosophila melanogaster* fruit fly. The fly naturally grows about thirty-six bristles, but Mayr was able to breed otherwise normal flies with as few as twenty-five and as many as fifty-six bristles. When Mayr pushed the fly's genetic material beyond these limits, samples became sterile and died out. When allowed to breed normally, though, even the most mutant strains returned to almost normal bristle counts within five generations.[25] Similarly, scientists have changed the famous peppered moth (*Briston betularia*) from speckled to silver, silver to black, and black back to speckled. But the moth never became green, purple, or blue; and it always remained a moth.[26]

In 1982 Francis Hitching reported, "Every series of breeding

---

[*] A heavy form of oxygen that coats the Earth's atmosphere in a thin, protective layer.

experiments that has ever taken place has established a finite limit to breeding possibilities."[27] He cited a remarkable series of tests in which mutant genes were paired to create an eyeless fly:

> When these flies in turn were interbred, the predictable result was offspring that were also eyeless. And so it continued for a few generations. But then, contrary to all expectations, a few flies began to hatch out with eyes. Somehow, the genetic code had a built-in repair mechanism that re-established the missing genes. The natural order reasserted itself.[28]

The fact that neither Darwin nor any subsequent biologist has ever succeeded in causing or even witnessing the evolution of one species into another[29] cannot help but disturb those who would like to believe in the theory of evolution.

The theoretical flaw that attracts the most attention in scientific circles, however, is the statistical one. When enough information about a certain event is available, scientists can determine just how likely that event is. In recent years biologists and mathematicians have been able to determine the probability of the random evolution of various life forms.

For example, Robert Shapiro, professor of chemistry at New York University, has estimated that the probability of randomly assembling a typical enzyme* (composed of two

---

* Electrons, protons, and neutrons are the building blocks of matter. When properly assembled, they form atoms, which in turn can be assembled into molecules. All chemicals are made of molecules, and certain chemicals (containing NH_2 and CO_2H groups) are called amino acids. Of the thousands of amino acids, nature uses only twenty (called "L-form amino acids") to construct proteins and enzymes. Finally, proteins and enzymes are the building blocks of bacteria, viruses, fungi, plants, fish, birds, animals, and people—all living things.

hundred linked L-form amino acids) in a single try is approximately 1 in 10^{20}.[30] In other words, this case is statistically comparable to randomly pulling a single red marble out of a mountain of 10^{20} black marbles in one try.

The odds of success increase, though, when we take into account the number of possible trials. The Earth is very large and very old. If we assume that L-form amino acid stew once covered the surface of the Earth to a depth of ten kilometers (about six miles) and that reactions could take place in every cubic micron* of the stew, we would then have 5×10^{36} separate reaction flasks. If we accept the fossil evidence, then a maximum of one billion years (about 3×10^{16} seconds) was available for the evolution of life on Earth.** If a separate try was made in every flask, every second, for a billion years, then the odds of randomly assembling a typical enzyme would be better than 99.99%.***

But an enzyme is far from life. A typical bacterium (which is life) is made of about two thousand different enzymes. To calculate the odds of randomly assembling such a bacterium from all the right enzymes, we take the probability of randomly assembling one enzyme and multiply that number by

---

* A micron is one-millionth of a meter, or 0.00003937 inches. A sheet of paper is about two hundred microns thick.

** Shapiro points out that since enzymes precede life, a billion years is a very generous ceiling for the amount of time enzymes had to form (p. 126).

*** $(5 \times 10^{36}$ reaction flasks$) \times (3 \times 10^{16}$ seconds$) = 1.5 \times 10^{53}$ total tries possible. Since the probability of any event $= 1 - (Y/[X+Y])^Z$ (where $X =$ the number of outcomes that would be considered successes, $Y =$ the number of outcomes that would be considered failures, and $Z =$ the number of possible trials), the probability of an enzyme evolving on earth $=$
$$1 - (10^{20}/[1+10^{20}])^{(1.5 \times 10^{53})} = \text{better than } 99.99\%.$$

itself two thousand times. The result: there is only a 1 in $10^{39,950}$ chance that a single viable bacterium ever evolved on Earth.* Remember: This is after we take into account a billion years' worth of trials. Calculations like this led Harold P. Klein, chairman of the National Academy of Sciences Committee on Origin-of-Life Research, to comment, "The simplest bacteria is so...complicated from the point of view of a chemist that it is almost impossible to imagine how it happened."[31]

In 1981, Nobel laureate Hoyle and his associate Wickramasinghe calculated that these odds constituted "[such] an outrageously small probability that [it] could not be faced even if the whole universe consisted of organic soup."[32] Hoyle added that it was more likely that "a tornado sweeping through a junkyard might assemble a Boeing 747 from the materials therein."[33]**

And these are the odds of just a single bacterium randomly evolving. The odds of several bacteria evolving are worse, and the probabilities that a virus or fungus would evolve are simply comical. What about people? There are 25,000 operative enzymes in a human being (in contrast to a bacterium's 2,000). The probability of 25,000 enzymes forming spontaneously once in a billion years is about 1 in $10^{599,950}$.*** In other words, the chances of *just the enzymes* in a person

---

* Giving Y a value of $(10^{20})^{2,000} = 10^{40,000}$, the probability of a typical bacterium evolving once in one billion years =

$$1 - (10^{40,000}/[1 + 10^{40,000}])^{(1.5 \times 10^{53})} = 10^{-39,950}.$$

** In February 1991, *Scientific American* reprinted Hoyle's comment, adding, "Most researchers agree with Hoyle on this point" (p. 102).

*** Giving Y a value of $(10^{20})^{25,000} = 10^{500,000}$, the probability of the evolution of a human's 25,000 enzymes during one billion years =

$$1 - (10^{500,000}/[1 + 10^{500,000}])^{(1.5 \times 10^{53})} = 10^{-599,950}.$$

evolving randomly sometime in Earth's history are the same as the chances of pulling one red marble out of a mound of black marbles *trillions and trillions and trillions times larger than the entire universe in one try*. And this is not to mention assembling those enzymes into skin, bones, muscles, eyes, noses, and ears, or assembling nucleotides into a strip of human DNA.*

The number $10^{599,950}$ is incomprehensibly large. This book contains only about 10^5 characters. A forest covering a million square miles, with ten thousand trees per square mile, and with one-hundred thousand leaves per tree, would contain only about 10^{15} leaves. The universe has only existed for at most 10^{18} seconds and contains only about 10^{80} atomic particles.[34] *Impossible* is only barely too strong a word to describe an event with a probability of 1 in $10^{599,950}$. Yet these odds are one of the most liberal estimates offered by scientists today.

Many experts believe that the probability that humans evolved is much slimmer. New York University's Robert Shapiro, for example, considers even a probability of 1 in $10^{39,950}$ for production of a bacterium to be too optimistic. "In fact, things are much worse," he wrote in 1986. "A tidy set of twenty amino acids, all in the L-form, was not likely to be available on the early Earth."[35] Instead, Shapiro endorses the probabilities calculated by Dr. Harold Morowitz, a Yale University physicist. Morowitz says there is one chance in $10^{100,000,000,000}$ that a viable bacterium ever evolved on Earth. Shapiro observes, "This number is so large that to write it in conventional form we would require several hundred thousand blank books."[36] And if the odds of evolution producing

---

* Barrow and Tipler say the odds of randomly assembling pre-made nucleotides into a human genome are between 1 in $10^{12,000,000}$ and 1 in $10^{24,000,000}$ (p. 565).

a *bacterium* are 1 in $10^{100,000,000,000}$, then the odds of producing a human being are closer to 1 in $10^{1,250,000,000,000}$—about the same as the odds of a gambler, using ordinary dice, rolling 100 trillion consecutive double-sixes.

Faced with such awe-inspiring statistics, the scientific world is reevaluating its approach to evolution. Thus, in 1966, at a University of Pennsylvania symposium entitled "Mathematical Challenges to the Neo-Darwinian Interpretation of Evolution," Professor Murray Eden of the Massachusetts Institute of Technology admitted, "An adequate scientific theory of evolution must await the discovery and elucidation of new natural laws—physical, physico-chemical and biological."[37] At the same conference, Marcel P. Schutzenberger of the University of Paris similarly disclosed, "We believe that there is a considerable gap in the neo-Darwinian theory of evolution, and we believe this gap to be of such a nature that it cannot be bridged within the current conception of biology."[38] In 1970 Professor Ernst Chain, a Nobel Prize-winning drug researcher, stated, "To postulate that the development and survival of the fittest is entirely a consequence of chance mutations seems to me a hypothesis based on no evidence and irreconcilable with the facts."[39] In 1978 Dr. John Keosian, with the Massachusetts Marine Biological Laboratory, published a work entitled *The Crisis in the Problem of the Origin of Life*, in which he concluded, "All present approaches to a solution of the problem of the origin of life are either irrelevant or lead into a blind alley. Therein lies the crisis."[40]

In 1973, Dr. Francis Crick, a Cambridge University professor who received the Nobel Prize for DNA research, admitted that life could not have evolved on Earth and must have been "sent here long ago in the form of germinal material, from elsewhere in the universe."[41] Crick's solution, the most rational he could muster given the barrage of defeats neo-Darwinism has suffered, was attacked as cheap science fiction. Crick held out, despite criticism, and was joined in 1978 by Sir Fred Hoyle and Dr. Chandra Wickramasinghe.

Hoyle and Wickramasinghe joined Crick in abandoning evolution in favor of "the seeding of space by intelligent beings from distant corners of the universe."[42] *Newsweek* mocked this thesis, reporting that "a biologist and an astronomer have performed the improbable feat of reinventing religion,"[43] and ultimately the two eminent scientists retracted major sections of their theory. But they still maintain that the theory of evolution has been disproved. Hoyle and Wickramasinghe wrote in 1981:

> No matter how large the environment one considers, life cannot have had a random beginning. Troops of monkeys thundering away at random on typewriters could not produce the works of Shakespeare, for the practical reason that the whole observable universe is not large enough to contain the necessary monkey hordes, the necessary typewriters, and certainly the waste paper baskets required for the deposition of wrong attempts. The same is true for living material.[44]

Wickramasinghe proclaimed in a 1984 interview:

> It does not follow logically that one can start from an organic soup and end up with a living system. There's no logic that drives you to that conclusion at all. And when we looked at the probabilities of the assembly of organic materials into a living system, it turns out that the improbabilities are really horrendous, horrific in extent, and I concluded along with my colleague [Sir Fred Hoyle] that [this] could not have happened spontaneously on the Earth.[45]

And in 1991, a *Scientific American* staff writer summed up the current state of origin-of-life research, quoting Crick, "The origin of life appears to be almost a miracle."[46]

In theory, of course, Darwinian evolution could someday explain the design apparent in human beings. Evidence of both the prebiotic soup and missing links might turn up. The apparently contradictory data (of organs that could not have evolved) might be explained away. The theoretical problems involved in maintaining an unstable prebiotic soup and stretching DNA past its mutability limits might be overcome. And then, having resolved all these difficulties, the components necessary to build a human being could theoretically exist as the result of an outrageous fluke—an event whose odds would range between 1 in $10^{599,950}$ and 1 in $10^{1,250,000,000,000}$. But we still would be unable to explain how all those components became DNA, eyes, ears, and noses; neither would we know what process transforms dead tissue into living beings.

III.

Stephen Hawking, a theoretical physicist at Cambridge University, wrote in 1988, "The whole history of science has been the gradual realization that events do not happen in an arbitrary manner, but that they reflect a certain underlying order."[47] The cause of that order remains a mystery today. The theory of evolution cannot realistically explain the existence of complex living things. Neither are there persuasive explanations for why astronomy, chemistry, and physics conspire day after day to provide mankind with such an ideal home. As of this writing, the natural answers to the teleological dilemma have failed. One can refuse to consider the supernatural solution, hoping that science will someday solve the conundrum. Or one can certainly find in the teleological perspective legitimate permission to believe.

NOTES

1. Denton, *Evolution: A Theory in Crisis* (Bethesda: Adler and Adler Publishers, Inc., 1986), p. 336.
2. Ibid., p. 334.
3. John D. Barrow and Frank J. Tipler, *The Anthropic Cosmological Principle* (Oxford: Clarendon Press, 1987), pp. 567-569.
4. Stephen W. Hawking, *A Brief History of Time* (New York: Bantam Books, 1988), pp. 121-122.
5. Barrow and Tipler, pp. 322-326.
6. Ibid., p. 336.
7. Denton, p. 261.
8. A. I. Oparin, ed., *Origin of Life* (Tokyo: Japan Scientific Societies Press, 1978), p. 604.
9. New York: Harper and Row, 1978, p. 26.
10. Sixth ed. (New York: Collier Books, 1962), p. 462.
11. Heribert-Nilsson, *Synthetische Artbildung*, 1954, cited by Francis Hitching, *The Neck of the Giraffe: Where Darwin Went Wrong* (New York: Ticknor and Fields, 1982), p. 22.
12. Ibid.
13. Raup, "Conflicts Between Darwin and Paleontology," *Bulletin* (Field Museum of Natural History) 50 (January 1979).
14. Ibid.
15. Denton, p. 162.
16. P. 182.
17. Tillyard, *The Biology of Dragonflies* (Cambridge University Press, 1917), p. 215.
18. Lloyd, *The Carnivorous Plants* (Waltham: Chronica Botanica Co., 1942), p. 7.
19. Wardlaw, *Organization and Evolution in Plants* (London: Longmans, Green and Co., Ltd., 1965), p. 405.
20. Chandler, *Introduction to Parasitology*, 10th ed. (New York: J. Wiley and Sons, 1961), p. 16.
21. Stahl, *Vertebrate History: Problems in Evolution* (New York: McGraw-Hill Book Co., 1974), p. 349.
22. Hitching, p. 88.

23. Ibid., p. 65.

24. Robert Shapiro, *Origins* (New York: Summit Books, 1986), pp. 112-113.

25. Norman Macbeth, *Darwin Retried* (Boston: Gambit Incorporated, 1971), p. 34.

26. Denton, pp. 79-81.

27. Hitching, p. 55.

28. Ibid., p. 57.

29. Denton, p. 55.

30. Shapiro, p. 127.

31. John Horgan, "In the Beginning: Trends in Evolution," *Scientific American*, February 1991, p. 104.

32. Hoyle and Wickramasinghe, *Evolution from Space* (London: J. M. Dent and Sons, 1981), p. 24.

33. Shapiro, p. 127.

34. Denton, p. 225. Also see Anthony Zee, *Fearful Symmetry: The Search for Beauty in Modern Physics* (New York: Macmillan Publishing, 1986), pp. 18, 289-290.

35. Shapiro, p. 127.

36. Ibid., p. 128.

37. Hitching, p. 83.

38. Ibid., p. 83.

39. Ibid., p. 82.

40. Oparin, ed., p. 574.

41. Ibid., p. 570. See also John Horgan, "In the Beginning: Trends in Evolution," *Scientific American*, February 1991, p. 102.

42. *Newsweek*, 1 March 1982, p. 55.

43. Ibid.

44. Hoyle and Wickramasinghe, *Evolution from Space*, p. 148.

45. "Science and the Divine Origin of Life," in *Intellectuals Speak Out About God*, ed. Roy A. Varghese (Chicago: Regnery Gateway Inc., 1984), p. 26.

46. John Horgan, "In the Beginning: Trends in Evolution," *Scientific American*, February 1991, p. 109.

47. Hawking, p. 122.

You have seen what I [God] did to Egypt, and how I bore you on eagles' wings and brought you to Me. Now, therefore, if you will obey My voice indeed and keep My covenant, then you will be My own treasure from among all peoples, for all the earth is Mine.

Exodus 19:4-5

CHAPTER FIVE

THE JEWISH HISTORY
APPROACH
TO GOD'S EXISTENCE

THOUSANDS OF YEARS ago, the Middle East, the cradle of civilization, was a hotbed of polytheism. Monotheism was completely unknown.[1] While most tribes recognized the existence of three to six gods, some groups, like the Ugarit, worshipped more than thirty.[2] From ancient man's perspective, polytheism must have seemed the most rational of belief systems. Man examined his environment, recognized the existence of forces beyond his understanding and control, and related to those forces as conscious creatures. It was monotheism—the belief that all the apparently disparate forces in the universe obey a single omnipotent, omniscient being—that seemed irrational.

For whatever reason, the Jews opposed all of mankind and declared the irrational to be true.* They set about spreading their idea, and, though it has taken time, they have enjoyed some success. As Drs. H. Frankfort, John Wilson, Thorkild Jacobsen, and William Irwin explained in a 1946 lecture sponsored by the University of Chicago:

> [Ancient] Israel's great achievement, so apparent that mention of it is almost trite, was monotheism. It was an achievement that transformed subsequent history.... With some entail of that danger always implicit in superlatives, one may raise the question whether any other single contribution from whatever source since human culture emerged from the stone ages has had the far-reaching effect upon history that [ancient] Israel in this regard has exerted, both through the mediums of Christianity and Islam and directly through the world of Jewish thinkers themselves.[3]

Monotheism remains the cornerstone of Judaism,** and the Jews, now joined by other religious groups who view the Torah as a Divine document, continue their effort to spread the idea that there is one God.

The question that perplexes historians is: *How did the Jews survive to enjoy the success they have?*

---

* Henry Bamford Parkes (with the New York University History Department) points out that "while a historical account illuminates the development of Jewish monotheism, it does not wholly explain it; other Near Eastern peoples were confronted by similar problems, but failed to make any comparable response" (p. 86).

** Contemporary religious Jews declare God's oneness aloud twice daily and pray three times a day for the era when God's oneness will be known by all mankind. See, for example, *The Complete Artscroll Siddur*, Rabbi Nosson Scherman, ed. (New York: Mesorah Publications, Ltd., 1984), pp. 90, 158, 984.

I.

We know that the Jews were but one of countless peoples that inhabited the primitive Middle East; and we can reasonably assume that, like today, survival of the fittest was the ethic that dominated international relations. But while neighboring groups evaporated through assimilation or were wiped out in inter-tribal skirmishes, the Jews endured.

They emerged from prehistory only to slip into Egyptian slavery. The Jews suffered, along with other small groups living near the Nile delta,[4] what must have been a gruesome bondage. The remnants of the massive grain storage facilities and tombs built by the pharaohs' slaves at Pithom and Raamses can be viewed today in modern Egypt, at Tell er-Rataba in Wadi Tummilat (outside of Cairo) and near San el-Hagar, a small fishing village on the Tanatic arm of the Nile.[5] Tens of thousands died in Egyptian service, an end the Jews escaped by fleeing into the Sinai desert around 1300 B.C.E.[6]

Historians are at a loss to explain how the Jews managed to get out of Egypt. Archaeologists are beginning to suspect that they slipped out amid a series of natural disasters that convulsed ancient Egypt. The *Ipuwer Papyrus*, acquired by the Museum of Leiden in 1828, contains an ancient Egyptian's eyewitness report of such disasters—the Nile flowing with blood, hail storms that devastated Egypt's crops, inexplicable darkness, and other strange phenomena.[7] A monolith discovered in el-Arish, a town near the modern Egyptian-Israeli border, contains a similar report.[8]

The problem historians face, even in light of such discoveries, stems from the widespread belief among Near Eastern scholars that the Jews were the only slave-people ever to escape Egyptian bondage.[9] How did the Jews get out during the disasters when no other peoples held by the pharaohs were able to get away?

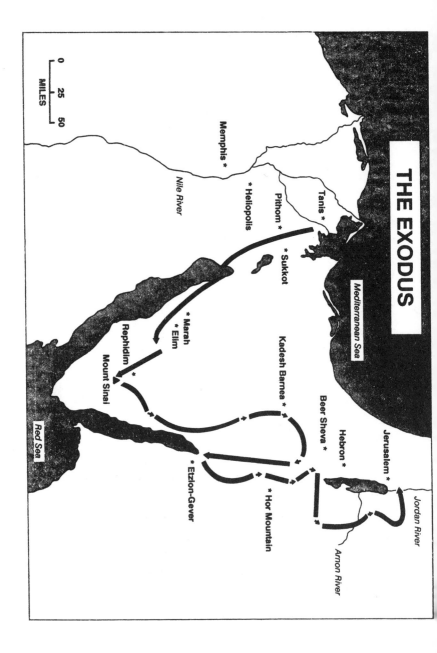

THE EXODUS

Mediterranean Sea

Memphis *

Nile River

* Heliopolis

Pithom *

Tanis *

* Sukkot

Rephidim
* Marah
* Elim

Mount Sinai

Kadesh Barnea *

Beer Sheva *

Hebron *

Jerusalem *

Jordan River

Arnon River

* Etzion-Gever

* Hor Mountain

Red Sea

0
25
50
MILES

The Jews proceeded into the perilous wilderness east of Egypt, where, in all probability, they were attacked by armed nomads and desert kings like those described in the biblical record.[10] They nevertheless arrived intact less than half a century later[11] at the border of what they believed was their Promised Land.

II.

The land that the Jews felt belonged to them was then occupied by more than a half-dozen nations. The archaeological record, in consonance with the book of Joshua, suggests that the Jews triumphed over the natives in a series of wildly destructive battles. Commenting on the findings of archaeologist Kathleen Kenyon at the biblical site of Jericho (the first town conquered by the Jews), a journalist reported, "Owing to erosion, the Kenyon researches threw no light on how the [city] walls were destroyed; [but] Kenyon thinks it may have been an earthquake, which the Israelites attributed to Divine intervention."[12] Similar ruins were found at the biblical sites of Gibeon and Hazor,[13] also towns taken by the Jews in their initial foray.

The Jews held the land of Israel for a time, repelling attack after attack from neighboring armies. In 701 B.C.E. the Assyrian king Sennacherib made it as far as the walls of Jerusalem, but his entire battalion was wiped out one night in a mysterious epidemic. The Greek historian Herodotus attributed the Assyrian defeat to "a violent outbreak of bubonic plague."[14] The biblical version of the story reads: "And it came to pass that night that the angel of the Lord went out and smote in the camp of Assyria one hundred eighty-five thousand; and when [the Jews] arose early in the morning, behold, [the Assyrians] were all dead corpses."[15]

The Jews held out until Nebuchadnezzar, king of Babylon, having crushed the Assyrian and Egyptian armies, swept down into Israel, demolished the Temple in Jerusalem, wrecked most of the homes in the region, murdered women and children on sight, and deported the survivors. The resulting exile, which historians date as commencing around 586 B.C.E., scattered the Jewish remnant across Babylon, Samaria, Edom, Moab, and Egypt. A remarkable history should have ended with the Babylonian exile: the Jews, like so many peoples who have been driven from their homelands, should have been swallowed up by their host cultures and assimilated out of existence.

III.

Seventy years later, though, there were still Jews in Babylon and the surrounding territories who cared about being Jewish. And when the Babylonian empire was uprooted by an alliance of Persians and Medes, the new head of state, Cyrus the Great, proclaimed the Jews free to return to Israel. News of the exile's end spread quickly, drawing waves of Jewish pilgrims from across the Near East. Under close Persian scrutiny, the Jews reestablished their independence and reconstructed their Temple in Jerusalem. They thus became the first people in recorded history to regain a land they had lost in a bloody defeat more than half a century earlier.

In 332 B.C.E. the Greeks completed a quick, lethal campaign against the Persian empire. Alexander of Macedon's generals carved up the Near East, establishing kingdoms in Egypt, Syria, Mesopotamia, and Anatolia. The Jews struggled to maintain some freedoms, despite the Greek stranglehold tightening around their community. But in 167 B.C.E. the Greeks outlawed Judaism and Jewish educational activities, and converted the Temple in Jerusalem into a showplace for Greek idols. The Jews moved to revolt but were put down by merciless troops. They then went underground, breaking into bands of guerrillas who would ravage the Greeks in and around the Temple area and then disappear into the Judean hills to regroup. Headed by Matisyahu Hasmon, the Jewish offensive caused the Greeks tremendous losses, and eventually the empire withdrew from Jerusalem. In 164 B.C.E. the Jews reclaimed their Temple and rededicated it to the one God. A tiny band of guerrillas had repelled the most powerful military force on the face of the globe.

As Greece withdrew, Rome quietly expanded its empire around Israel. In 40 B.C.E., having replaced Greece as the preeminent world power, the Romans dispatched an army of 30,000 infantry and 6,000 cavalry to take Jerusalem. In sheer military might the Romans dwarfed the Jews. The battle was over before it began, and the Romans installed Herod as "allied king and friend of the Roman people."[16] Herod's primary goal was to exterminate the Jewish guerrillas who had so troubled the Greeks. He largely succeeded, and celebrated his victory in 37 C.E. by executing forty-six leading members of the Sanhedrin (the Jews' supreme religious council). Having disposed of his Jewish opponents, Herod tried to placate the remaining Jewish populace, even going so far as to begin rebuilding the Temple.

Herod died in 44 C.E., and though the Romans were pleased with his compromise approach, they lacked a replacement who could mollify the Jewish populace while maintaining solid Roman control. Thus, Rome saw no choice but to impose direct rule over Jerusalem, which it did immediately. It took the Jews until 46 C.E. to muster the manpower and armaments for their first rebellion, which was put down quickly. Their next revolt, however, in 66 C.E. almost succeeded and triggered a massive Roman response. Four full legions descended on Jerusalem.[17] Hundreds of Jews were crucified weekly. Jewish scholars were flayed alive. Torah scrolls was burned publicly. The Temple was ransacked and razed to rubble. Survivors fled from the area. The end of the Jewish state was at hand, and the end of the Jewish people should not have lagged far behind.

But it did. The Jews defied history and endured.

IV.

The rough times for the Jewish people were not over, though. In 135 C.E. a failed Jewish revolt near Jerusalem led to a Roman-orchestrated orgy of worldwide anti-Semitism that left 580,000 Jews dead and 985 towns devastated.[18] In 470 C.E. Persia's Emperor Firiz initiated a national campaign to destroy the Jews, exterminating half the Jewish population of Ipahan.[19]

Jews who found themselves strewn across Europe were subjected to centuries of vicious Christian anti-Semitism, culminating in the Crusades (1095-1348 C.E.). During these bloody years, Christians on holy pilgrimage to Jerusalem slaughtered thousands of Jews at a time. Hundreds of Jewish communities were decimated.[20]

When the Black Death (bubonic plague) struck Europe between 1347 and 1350, both the Church and the peasantry blamed the Jews, and anti-Semitism escalated. Between 1348 and 1354, thousands of European Jewish communities were massacred.[21] Some Jews fled to Spain and Poland. Poland remained safe for a period but in Spain, between 1366 and 1500, the Catholic church consolidated its power by stirring the masses into anti-Semitic frenzies. The result was the Spanish Inquisition, during which Jewish property was confiscated, synagogues and Jewish literature were burned, and Jews fell prey to forced conversions and mass murder.[22]

There were still Jews alive in 1648 when revolution rocked northern Europe. The Polish army's defeat by an alliance of Cossacks and Tartars brought to power Bogdan

Chmielnicki, a Cossack with an ingenious plan for uniting the Ukraine. Chmielnicki enlisted the peasantry into the most appalling series of pogroms the Jews had ever experienced. Bands of Cossacks traveled from city to city in search of Jews, whom they murdered in perversely cruel ways. Yet Chmielnicki succeeded in wiping out only one-third of Polish Jewry before a new Polish king, John Casimir, exiled the remaining Jews from Chernigov, Poltava, Kiev, and parts of Poldolia.[23] Twenty thousand Jews fled to the Swedish border, only to be murdered in 1656 when Polish troops, repelling a Swedish invasion, took time out to destroy Posen, Kalish, Cracow, Piotrkovthe, and other Jewish settlements.[24]

Small groups of Jews around the world were the targets of constant lootings, rapes, and murders in the years leading up to the twentieth century. Somehow, though, the Jews were spared total annihilation.

V.

In 1915 Grand Duke Nicholas, commander-in-chief of the Russian army, ordered the relocation of all Jews living in any area ever occupied by the German army. One hundred thousand Jews were murdered in the deportations. In 1917, following Russia's October revolution, Ukrainians and White Russians joined forces to massacre 200,000 more Jews. In the next two years, another 120,000 Jews died in almost five hundred pogroms.[25]

Adolf Hitler, a rising German politician, gave his first speech concerning the Jews on August 13, 1920.[26] In 1925 he published Mein Kampf, a lengthy document that detailed the "program of blood and terror"[27] he one day hoped to conduct against the Jews. In 1930, anti-Semitic riots broke out in Berlin, Wurzberg, Leipzig, Dusseldorf, and Frankfurt.[28] In the first months of 1933, Jews were attacked and beaten publicly, and that April, Hitler barred them from public service as well as from the legal, medical, and academic professions.[29] Before the end of 1933, Dachau, Germany's first "concentration camp," was established on the outskirts of Munich.[30] In 1935, the Reich Citizenship Act stripped all Jews of their German citizenship.[31] In 1938, Hitler inaugurated "concentration camps" at Sachsenhausen, Buchenwald, and Lichtenburg.[32] Thirty thousand Jews were herded off to the camps.[33]

On the morning of November 9, 1938, Reich Minister for Propaganda Josef Goebbels announced a state-sanctioned anti-Jewish campaign, and that night thousands of Jewish shops were vandalized, thousands of shopowners beaten, and countless synagogues burned.[34] On September 1, 1939, Hitler created the Einsatzgruppen, death squads that conducted a door-to-door campaign against Jews found behind enemy lines. Jews within German-controlled areas were tortured in medical experiments, raped, mutilated, machine-gunned into mass graves, and gassed. In the following months Germany established hundreds of extermination centers across Europe. More than two-thirds of European Jewry—nearly six million people—were obliterated before Germany's defeat in 1945.[35] Had Hitler won the war, there would be no Jews today.

VI.

In 1948, for the first time in recorded human history, a people twice exiled from its land returned to establish an independent state. On May 14 of that year, the State of Israel was created. The following day, five mechanized Arab armies descended on the ragged band of Holocaust survivors who populated the new country. Armed with only 17,600 rifles, 2,700 sten-guns, and 1,000 machine guns, fewer than 45,000 Jews faced the combined military forces of Egypt, Syria, Iraq, Lebanon and Transjordan.[36] Azzam Pasha, secretary-general of the Arab League, proclaimed over the airways, "This will be a war of extermination and a momentous massacre."[37] Indeed, it should have been. But in a performance that conjured up visions of their ancestors' biblical victories, the Jews held the Arabs off. Less than a month after the war broke out, the United Nations declared a cease-fire. It appeared that there would be a third Jewish state.

In July 1951, King Abdullah of Jordan, the last of the Arab moderates, was assassinated. One year later a military junta ousted the Egyptian monarchy, leading to the reign of Gamal Abdul Nasser, a vicious anti-Semite bent on Israel's destruction. In 1953 Stalin broke off Soviet relations with Israel, and within two years Soviet weapons were pouring into Arab munitions depots. In 1956, having already blocked Israeli access to the Suez Canal and the Gulf of Aquaba, a confident Nasser signed military pacts with Saudi Arabia and Yemen, formed a unified military command with Jordan and Syria, and stepped up *fedayeen* attacks on Israeli settlements. War was imminent when, on October 29, 1956, Israel launched a preemptive raid on the terrorist units in the Sinai. To their surprise, the Israelis quickly took the Egyptian outposts of Rafa, el-Arish, the Gaza Strip, the coasts of the Suez Canal and the Gulf of Aquaba, and Sharm el-Sheikh. Just over a week after the war began, on November 7, the United Nations' cease-fire order was accepted, but only after the Israelis had confirmed their uncanny ability to defend themselves even against the latest Soviet weapons.

As part of the 1956 peace settlement, in a move unprecedented in military history, Israel gave back most of the territory it had conquered. The Sinai was to remain demilitarized under Egyptian control.

In 1967, an impatient Nasser violated the truce by moving 100,000 troops into the Sinai. On May 15, he ordered the withdrawal of the United Nations peacekeeping units, which

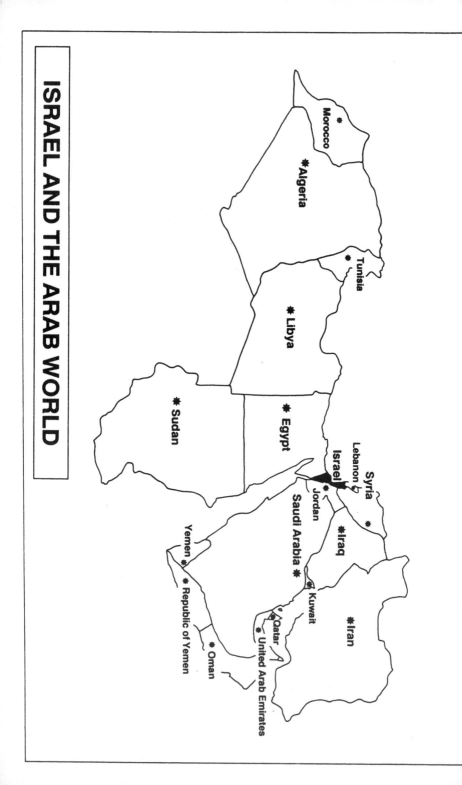

ISRAEL AND THE ARAB WORLD

Morocco

Algeria

Tunisia

Libya

Sudan

Egypt

Lebanon

Israel

Syria

Jordan

Saudi Arabia

Iraq

Yemen

Kuwait

Iran

Qatar

Republic of Yemen

United Arab Emirates

Oman

complied instantly.[38] On May 22, Nasser blockaded the Gulf of Aquaba, and eight days later he signed a military pact with King Hussein of Jordan. The same day, under Jordanian guidance, Iraqi forces took positions on the Israeli-Jordanian border.

On June 5, reacting to intelligence reports that war was again imminent, Israel launched a preemptive strike. In a single day, it destroyed the entire Egyptian air force.[39] Jordan and Syria both declared war. In six days Israel defeated all three armies, each many times the size of its own. The Israelis retook the Sinai, captured Jerusalem (which was lost in 1948), pushed into Syria's Golan Heights, and planted troops thirty miles outside of Damascus. To this day world military experts are at a loss to explain the Jews' 1967 victory.

Terrorist attacks on Israel continued regularly after 1967, but its borders were secure. Until 1973.

That year, on Yom Kippur, the holiest day of the Jewish year, while most Israelis filled the country's synagogues, Egypt and Syria again endeavored to annihilate the Jewish state. This time they penetrated Israeli lines, and Soviet-supplied anti-tank and anti-aircraft missiles eased their move across the tiny country. Surprised and unprepared, Israel initially faltered. Journalists in the West wrote of the end of Israel and the coming holocaust. But again, this time within eighteen days, the Israelis were victorious and reestablished their borders. The world was rightfully astounded.

Today Israel suffers terrorist attacks almost daily. Still, the Jews have their state, a state they lost almost two thousand years ago. The people of Israel have resurrected Hebrew, the language of the Bible, a language once dead and now spoken by millions of Israelis and other Jews worldwide. Judaism flourishes both in Israel and in the diaspora. Tens of thousands of Jews, estranged from their religious heritage by the horrors of Jewish history, have returned to the faith of their fathers.* Jewish seminaries around the world are overflowing with new students. The Jews and Judaism, respectively the longest-lived nation and religion in human history,** are alive and well against outrageous odds.

VII.

Paul Johnson, formerly a writer for the *New York Times* and now editor of the *New Statesman*, recorded the following thoughts while touring Israel:

> When the historian visits Hebron today, he asks himself: Where are all those peoples which once held the place? Where are the Canaanites? Where are the Edomites? Where are the ancient Hellenes and the Romans, the Byzantines, the Franks, the Mamluks and the Ottomans? They have vanished into time, irrevocably. But the Jews are still in Hebron.[40]

All the great powers who sought to wipe out the Jews throughout history are themselves gone. But the Jews remain

---

* In 1982 American demographers reported over 11,000 full-time yeshiva students in the United States alone. A year later, Israeli demographers reported a national yeshiva enrollment of about 53,000. A study two years later indicated that another 14,000 married men were studying in graduate institutions called *kollelim*. It is now thought that more than a quarter of a million Jews worldwide participate in a daily Talmud study program of some sort. See *With Fury Poured Out*, Bernard Maza (Hoboken: Ktav Publishing House, 1986), pp. 175-223.

** Abraham, the first of the Jewish people's forefathers, lived approximately 1,700 years before the beginning of the common era and about 1,200 years before the founding of Buddhism, Confucianism, Hinduism, and Taoism. See *Religions East and West*, Ward J. Fellows (Ft. Worth: Holt, Rinehart and Winston, 1979).

and thrive. All peoples pass in and out of existence. But the Jews defy history. Even Soviet historian Nicolas Berdyaev said of the Jews during a lecture to the Moscow Liberal Academy of Spiritual Culture: "...their destiny is too imbued with the metaphysical to be explained in either material or positive-historical terms."[41] He further confessed:

> I remember how the materialist interpretation of history, when I attempted in my youth to verify it by applying it to the destinies of peoples, broke down in the case of the Jews, where destiny seemed absolutely inexplicable from the materialistic standpoint. And, indeed, according to the materialistic and positivist criterion, this people ought long ago to have perished.[42]

In 1897, Mark Twain wrote of the Jews:

> If the statistics are right, the Jews constitute but one percent of the human race. It suggests a nebulous dim puff of stardust lost in the blaze of the Milky Way. Properly the Jew ought hardly to be heard of; but he is heard of, has always been heard of. He is as prominent on the planet as any other people....He has made a marvelous fight in this world, in all the ages; and he has done it with his hands tied behind him....The Egyptian, the Babylonian, and the Persian rose, filled the planet with sound and splendor, then faded to dreamstuff and passed away; the Greek and the Roman followed, and made a vast noise, and they are gone; other peoples have sprung up and held their torch high for a time, but it burned out, and they sit in twilight now, or have vanished. The Jew saw them all, beat them all, and is now what he always was, exhibiting no decadence, no infirmities of age, no weaken-

ing of his parts, no slowing of his energies, no dulling of his alert and aggressive mind. All things are mortal but the Jew; all other forces pass, but he remains. What is the secret of his immortality?[43]

We feebly struggle to explain Jewish survival in secular terms: Maybe it is because they were poor? Maybe it is because they were rich? Maybe it is because they were pacifists? Maybe it is because they fought back? Maybe it is because they were concentrated? Maybe it is because they were scattered? But we know that other peoples shared these characteristics and are gone. The question stands: Why did only the Jews survive?

The theological solution is attractive.

VIII.

Still we are bothered: If the Jews merit some special Divine protection, then why have they suffered so terribly for so long? Is not the suffering of the Jews itself an argument against their God's existence?

The Bible answers this objection in two terrifying passages. First, God explains to the Jews:

> If you walk in My statutes and keep My commandments and do them, then I will give you rain in due season....And I will give you peace in the land, and you will lie down and no one will make you afraid; and I will remove evil beasts from the land, neither will the sword pass through your land....And I will walk among you and will be your God, and you shall be My people....
>
> But if you will not listen to Me and do all these commands...I will set My face against you and you will be killed before your enemies....I will also send wild

beasts among you, which will rob you of your children and destroy your cattle and make you few in number....And I will make your cities waste and bring your sanctuaries to desolation....And I will scatter you among the nations and draw a sword after you....And those who are left of you will pine away in their iniquity in your enemies' lands....[44]

Later, God predicts that His chosen people "will forsake Me and break My covenant, which I have made with them. Then My anger will burn against them on that day, and I will forsake them and hide My face from them, and they will be devoured...."[45] The Bible makes clear that the Jewish people's covenant with God works in two directions. To the extent that the Jews differentiate themselves from all other peoples by observing God's commandments, God places them above normal historical processes and preserves them. But, in the words of Rabbi Moshe Meiselman, a prominent Jerusalem-based Talmudic scholar: "The moment we begin treating ourselves as just another nation, then we, like them, become subject to natural processes. We become governed by the natural laws of history, and according to the laws of history, the Jewish people simply should not exist."[46]

When large segments of the Jewish people assimilate and leave their religious heritage behind, the Bible suggests, then the entire Jewish people will taste normality; then it will feel the pressure of that evolutionary force that drives peoples out of existence. Both the Talmud[47] and modern historians[48] confirm the spread of such assimilation prior to the destruction of both the first and second Temples in Jerusalem. Historian Lucy Dawidowicz writes that, Soviet Jewry aside, only about half of pre-World War II East European Jewry was observant, and "secularity was becoming the dominant mode."[49] Meiselman[50] cites Rabbi Meir Simcha Hacohen, who wrote in 1927, "Those people who said that Berlin is Jerusalem and that German is the chosen language were, according to the unique rules of Jewish history, setting the German people up to destroy us."

Finally we might object: Is it fair that a pocket of sincerely religious Jews must die just because most of their community has abandoned Judaism? Do not the deaths of the devout in the Holocaust and in other pogroms throughout history testify persuasively against God's existence?

So it would seem, unless pious Jews are held responsible for ignoring the spiritual needs of the less devout. The Talmud records that when the first Temple was destroyed, even the most righteous Jews were condemned for not reaching out to their assimilating compatriots.[51] Furthermore, those who are closest to the Almighty might be held to a higher standard. Maybe those with the clearest understanding of God's will are the most obligated to fulfill it and the most punishable for infractions. The Bible offers just such an explanation for the premature deaths of Moses' nephews, who deviated slightly in their Divine service and were instantly consumed in a heavenly fire.[52]

In short: The Jews can explain why the Jewish people has suffered; it is now incumbent upon humanity to explain why the Jewish people has survived. And one who feels dissatisfied with the non-religious responses to the riddle of Jewish endurance can certainly find in the history of this unusual people permission to believe.

NOTES

1. Michael Grant, *The History of Ancient Israel* (New York: Charles Scribner's Sons, 1984), pp. 21-26; Henry Bamford Parkes, *Gods and Men: The Origins of Western Culture* (New York: Alfred A. Knopf, 1959), pp. 85-98.

2. Grant, p. 22.

3. Frankfort, Wilson, Jacobsen, and Irwin, *The Intellectual Adventure of Ancient Man* (Chicago: University of Chicago Press, 1946), p. 224.

4. W. F. Albright, *From the Stone Age to Christianity* (Baltimore: Johns Hopkins University Press), pp. 254-255. Also see Werner Keller, *The Bible as History* (New York: William Morrow and Co., 1981), pp. 118-124; Grant, p. 37.

5. Paul Johnson, *A History of the Jews* (New York: Harper & Row, 1987), p. 25; Keller, p. 121.

6. Philip Biberfeld, *Universal Jewish History*, vol. I (New York: Spero Foundation, 1948), p. 30.

7. Immanuel Velikovsky, *Ages in Chaos*, vol. I (New York: Doubleday and Co. Inc., 1952), pp. 22-38.

8. Ibid., pp. 39-45.

9. Johnson, p. 26.

10. Numbers 14:45; 21:1, 23, 33.

11. Biberfeld, p. 31.

12. Johnson, p. 43.

13. Ibid., p. 44.

14. Johnson, p. 73.

15. II Kings 19:35.

16. Johnson, p. 110.

17. Ibid., p. 137.

18. Heinrich Hirsh Graetz, *A History of the Jews* (Philadelphia: Jewish Publication Society, 1898), pp. 407-419.

19. Paul E. Grosser and Edwin G. Halperin, *Anti-Semitism: Causes and Effects* (New York: Philosophical Library, 1978), p. 81.

20. Ibid., pp. 102-120.

21. Ibid., pp. 126-132.

22. Ibid., pp. 134-154.

23. S. M. Dubnow, *A History of the Jews in Russia and Poland: From the Earliest Times Until the Present Day* (Philadelphia: Jewish Publication Society, 1920), pp. 149-151.

24. Ibid., p. 156.

25. Abram Sachar, *A History of the Jews* (New York: Knopf Publishers, 1969), pp. 302-303.

26. Grosser and Halperin, pp. 249-250.

27. Konrad Heiden, introduction to Adolf Hitler, *Mein Kampf* (Boston: Houghton Mifflin Company, 1971), p. xv.

28. Marvin Lowenthal, *The Jews of Germany: A Story of Sixteen Centuries* (New York: Longmans, Green and Company, 1936), p. 375.

29. Martin Broszat, *Anatomy of the S.S. State* (Cambridge: William Collins Sons & Company, 1968), pp. 23-27; William Lawrence Shirer, *The Rise and Fall of the Third Reich* (Greenwich: Fawcett, 1950), pp. 283, 358.

30. Lucy S. Dawidowicz, *The War Against the Jews 1933-1945* (New York: Bantam Books, 1975), p. 100.

31. Broszat, p. 32.

32. Ibid., p. 445.

33. Ibid., pp. 41-42.

34. Ibid., pp. 40-41.

35. Dawidowicz, p. 544.

36. Johnson, pp. 526-527.

37. Rony E. Gabbay, *A Political Study of the Arab Jewish Conflict* (Geneva, 1959), pp. 92-93, cited in Johnson, p. 526.

38. Johnson, p. 534.

39. Ibid.

40. Johnson, p. 4.

41. Berdyaev, *The Meaning of History* (New York: Charles Scribner's Sons, 1936), p. 86.

42. Ibid.

43. *The Complete Works of Mark Twain*, American Artists Edition (New York: Harper and Brothers, 1899), p. 286.

44. Leviticus 26:3-39.

45. Deuteronomy 31:16-17.

46. Meiselman, *Oraisa* (Jerusalem: Feldheim Publishers, 1989), p. 17.

47. Tractate *Yoma* 9b.

48. Johnson, pp. 72-149.
49. Dawidowicz, p. 335.
50. Meiselman, p. 19.
51. Tractate *Shabbos* 55a.
52. Leviticus 10:1-3.

For Job said, "I was righteous, yet God deprived me of justice."

Job 34:5

CHAPTER SIX

WHY BAD THINGS HAPPEN TO GOOD PEOPLE

FOR MANY, THE last obstacle in the path towards belief is the simple yet disturbing observation that good people sometimes suffer and evil people sometimes flourish. It seems obvious that an omnipotent, omniscient, moral God would not allow injustice. Upon witnessing inequity, it is therefore perfectly natural to doubt God's existence. Admittedly, this apparent injustice in the world is one of the most difficult concepts a believer must cope with; it is not, however, a proof that God does not exist.

I.

The first step in coming to terms with the inequity of reward and punishment is recognizing the extent of the problem. How much Divine injustice do we genuinely know about?

We must ask ourselves—and answer with cold, unemotional honesty—how many evil people we have seen enjoying life, and how many righteous people we have seen suffering. Such analysis requires access to two pieces of elusive information.

First, we must know who is good and who is evil. But as any historian, psychologist, or businessman will attest: The people most widely considered to be good are not necessarily good, and the people most widely thought to be evil are not necessarily evil. Indeed, the most evil people in history succeeded in their endeavors by maintaining a facade of altruism. Being evil often involves lying, presenting an upright, even saintly image. Both Hitler and Stalin, two of the most vile human beings ever to walk the planet, were known to their followers as heroic saviors. Goodness, in contrast, includes qualities like humility and modesty; and humble, modest people tend to hide their righteousness. Good people also sometimes sacrifice their personal reputation for higher values. For instance, the English monarchy viewed Thomas Jefferson, George Washington, and the other framers of the American Constitution as petty outlaws interested only in stealing land and inciting rebellion among British colonists. Yet these were men of vision.

Although Hitler, Stalin, Jefferson, and Washington are extreme examples, they nonetheless demonstrate how moral stature can be misunderstood. How many people do we know intimately enough to be certain that they do not deserve a particular reward or punishment? Do we know *with absolute certainty* what people do when they are away from us, what their motivations are, or what the outcome of their actions will be? The point here is not to slip into paranoid suspicion or unrealistic hero worship, but rather to recognize that in many cases we cannot definitively say that someone received an unfair lot in life.

The second piece of missing information is: What is

reward and what is punishment? After all, circumstances are not always what they appear to be. A man who wins an around-the-world airline ticket has not necessarily been rewarded. His flight might crash or be hijacked. Similarly, a woman forced to seek medical treatment has not necessarily been punished. She might end up falling in love with and marrying her physician. In addition, one man's punishment is another's reward. We might pity a man who gets stuck in a crowded elevator when it breaks down; but the man might relish the opportunity to forget about business for a few hours and meet some new people. Or we might envy a woman whose job takes her all around the world; but she might much rather spend time at home with friends and family.

Even after this limited analysis, then, we recognize how few cases there are of clear Divine injustice.

II.

The next step in coming to terms with apparent Divine injustice involves recognizing that if God exists, it is also possible that there is an entire non-physical world—a world unbound by time or space—and a soul, a human essence that survives death and passes into this eternal world. Human existence might actually be divided into two distinct segments—finite life and infinite afterlife—separated by an event called death.

Even most good people make a few moral errors, and even evil people occasionally act righteously. If God is absolutely just, He must reward every act of righteousness and punish every moral error. But when should God reward good people and punish evil ones? This world is finite. A physical, frail human being can experience only so much reward and punishment. In contrast, an afterlife could be infinite. An eternal soul could experience highs and lows that we, in our limited understanding, could not even begin to comprehend.

Is it not possible that God gives evil people some of their reward during the finite existence we call life, and reserves most of their punishment for eternal, infinite afterlife?* Likewise, perhaps God lets good people experience some of their punishment in this world, and reserves most of their reward for the eternal world to come? If God really exists, we might expect to see good people periodically suffering and evil people periodically flourishing, so that later, in an infinite world, good people can receive a purer, more intense reward and evil people a purer, more intense punishment.

The fact that good people suffer and evil people prosper thus remains a challenge only to one who would posit God's existence but reject the existence of a soul and an afterlife. Whatever injustice we experience or witness is comprehensible (at least intellectually)** to one who not only posits God's existence, but has also allowed for other spiritual potentialities.

---

* Judaism posits just such a system of justice. In fact, Rabbi Moses Maimonides, the most prominent of medieval Jewish legal authorities, lists belief in an afterlife among the thirteen essential principles of Jewish faith. (See Maimonides' introduction to his commentary on chapter 11 of tractate *Sanhedrin.*)

** Logic notwithstanding, people cannot be expected to accept apparent Divine injustice peaceably. Someone who has experienced real agony—or supported someone else who has—will take little comfort in intellectual explanations. Suffering afflicts the heart, and reason can only satisfy the mind. Someone whose life is touched by suffering will certainly ask: Why couldn't God, who is unbound by logic, have constructed existence differently? If God can do anything, let Him perform the apparently impossible: let Him eliminate suffering while preserving our free will! To such objections there is no rational response. To someone in pain we can offer only compassion.

III.

Finally, even for someone who would deny the existence of a soul and an afterlife, the seeming iniquity of reward and punishment does not represent a serious argument against God's existence. Any rational person will admit that, in theory, the ways of God could be so complex that they defy human understanding. Man might simply be incapable of comprehending and morally evaluating the behavior of an omniscient, omnipotent Being. Just as appropriate actions taken by a parent can sometimes seem unjustified to young children, God's actions might sometimes strike us as indefensible, despite their absolute righteousness. Our occasional inability to discern God's goodness is not a repudiation of His existence as much as a confession of our own intellectual finitude. Because man cannot be expected to grasp the mind of God, the fact that bad things happen to good people need not hinder those who seek permission to believe.

EPILOGUE

WE FIND OURSELVES in a perplexing world. Many of us sense that murder is wrong, but we do not know why. The universe apparently burst forth from nothingness, but we cannot describe how. Something seems to impose order upon all existence, but we do not know what. The Jewish people endures, and we cannot explain why.

We would like to answer these questions. We would like to make reality comprehensible. And so we struggle to construct a world view. We analyze the world and make assumptions to explain what we see. Scientists tell us that a good theory usually satisfies two requirements: it accounts for phenomena using a few reasonable assumptions, and it makes predictions that can be validated by observation.[1] Ideally any world view we assemble should do the same.

It is tempting to take the easiest path and adopt a world

view that attributes everything to chance, to absolute randomness. At least insofar as it would keep the theological issue at bay, it would be comforting to say that the universe and all it contains is simply a fortuitous fluke. But such an answer is flawed, for randomness cannot dictate that murder is wrong. Indeed, randomness does not allow for any system of moral absolutes. Moreover, randomness cannot justify the current belief among many scientists that the universe appeared out of nothing. Furthermore, even the events that could conceivably be attributed to randomness—like the formation of the solar system and the evolution of man—are ridiculously unlikely, even given the periods of time involved. Lastly, a theory based on randomness makes no disprovable predictions. Because it predicts that anything can happen, it can never be verified.

It is also tempting to avoid the theological issue by assembling a complex package of secular assumptions to account for phenomena like an ordered universe and the survival of the Jews. No matter how sophisticated, though, no such assumptions could ever generate the conclusion that murder is absolutely wrong. Furthermore, the set of assumptions we would need to explain reality would be outrageously large, and would include many suppositions that are at least as controversial as God's existence. For example, we would probably need to suggest that objects can appear out of nothing; that there is an as yet undetected ordering force; and that the Jewish people possesses some natural trait or set of traits that at least partially shields them from all destructive forces—natural, military, and demographic.

For the staunch agnostic, prospects are dim. The only remaining option is to posit God's existence. Worse yet, the theological solution meets the scientific criteria of a good theory. We can account for every aspect of reality by making the one assumption that a moral Creator/Designer chose the

Jews and gave them the Torah. Furthermore, we can generate verifiable predictions. We can predict, for example, that the Jewish people will never become extinct (as it says in Leviticus 26:44) that Jewish communities will enjoy peace and prosperity whenever they behave in accordance with the ethical and ritual guidelines of the Bible; and that they will suffer whenever they ignore these guidelines.

Of course, there is not yet a scientific or philosophical—mathematically incontestable—proof that the world view based on God is correct. Even scientifically sound theories can be wrong; and even outlandish, unprovable ones can be correct. Still, it seems sensible to choose the less complicated, more verifiable option.

Intelligent people do not require mathematically incontestable proof of God's existence any more than they require proof that there is a gravitational force, or that Abraham Lincoln once served as President of the United States. None of these theories is inarguable, yet all have accurately described our findings for so long that they have earned our confidence. Indeed, God's existence is among the longest lived, most widely accepted theories in history. It has captured the attention of great minds in great civilizations for millennia. And it is bolstered by more evidence than ever.

Despite the powerful case for God's existence, people cannot be expected to develop perfect belief solely by means of intellectual investigation. Perfect belief is a sublime spiritual achievement. It is an exquisite, overwhelming certainty that is not born overnight, and is not purely intellectual. Still, those who would start down the path towards perfect belief can only benefit from examining the intellectual case for God's existence. For those willing to take a long, honest look, the world is brimming with permission to believe.

NOTES

1. Stephen W. Hawking, *A Brief History of Time* (New York: Bantam Books, 1988), pp. 9-10.

BIBLIOGRAPHY

Albright, William Foxwell. *From the Stone Age to Christianity*. Baltimore: Johns Hopkins University Press, 1962.

Barrow, John D., and Frank J. Tipler. *The Anthropic Cosmological Principle*. Oxford: Clarendon Press, 1987.

Berdyaev, Nicolas. *The Meaning of History*. New York: Charles Scribner's Sons, 1936.

Biberfeld, Philip. *Universal Jewish History*. Vol. I. New York: Spero Foundation, 1948.

Broszat, Martin. *Anatomy of the S.S. State*. Cambridge: William Collins Sons & Co., 1968.

Chandler, Asa Crawford. *Introduction to Parasitology*. 10th ed. New York: J. Wiley and Sons, 1961.

Chandler, David. "Satellite's New Data Smoothly Supports Big Bang Theory." *Boston Sunday Globe*, 14 January 1990.

Darwin, Charles. *The Origin of Species*. 6th ed. New York: Collier Books, 1962.

Dawidowicz, Lucy S. *The War Against the Jews 1933-1945*. New York: Bantam Books, 1975.

Denton, Michael. *Evolution: A Theory in Crisis*. Bethesda: Adler and Adler Publishers, Inc., 1986.

Dubnow, S. M. *A History of the Jews in Russia and Poland: From the Earliest Times Until the Present Day*. Philadelphia: Jewish Publication Society, 1920.

Fellows, Ward J. *Religions East and West*. Ft. Worth: Holt, Rinehart and Winston, 1979.

Fisch, Harold, ed. *The Holy Scriptures*. Jerusalem: Koren Publishers, 1984.

Frankfort, H., John Wilson, Thorkild Jacobsen, and William Irwin. *The Intellectual Adventure of Ancient Man*. Chicago: University of Chicago Press, 1946.

Gilbert, Martin. *Auschwitz and the Allies*. London: Arrow Books Limited, 1984.

Graetz, Heinrich Hirsh. *A History of the Jews*. Philadelphia: Jewish Publication Society, 1898.

Grant, Michael. *The History of Ancient Israel*. New York: Charles Scribner's Sons, 1984.

Grosser, Paul E., and Edwin G. Halperin. *Anti-Semitism: Causes and Effects*. New York: Philosophical Library, 1978.

Hawking, Stephen W. *A Brief History of Time*. New York: Bantam Books, 1988.

Hitching, Francis. *The Neck of the Giraffe: Where Darwin Went Wrong*. New York: Tiknor and Fields, 1982.

Hitler, Adolf. *Mein Kampf*. Translated by Ralph Manheim. Boston: Houghton Mifflin Co., 1971.

Horgan, John. "In the Beginning: Trends in Evolution," *Scientific American*, February 1991.

———. "Trends in Cosmology," *Scientific American*, October 1990.

Hoyle, Fred, and Chandra Wickramasinghe. *Lifecloud*. New York: Harper & Row, 1978.

———. *Evolution from Space*. London: J. M. Dent and Sons, 1981.

Jastrow, Robert. *God and the Astronomers*. New York: Warner Books, 1984.

———. "Have Astronomers Found God?" *New York Times Magazine*, 25 June 1978.

Johnson, Paul. A History of the Jews. New York: Harper & Row, 1987.

Keller, Werner. The Bible as History. New York: William Morrow and Co., 1981.

Lloyd, Francis Ernest. The Carnivorous Plants. Waltham: Chronica Botanica Co., 1942.

Lowenthal, Marvin. The Jews of Germany: A Story of Sixteen Centuries. New York: Longmans, Green and Co., Ltd., 1936.

Macbeth, Norman. Darwin Retried. Boston: Gambit Incorporated, 1971.

Maza, Bernard. With Fury Poured Out. Hoboken: Ktav Publishing House, 1986.

Meiselman, Moshe. Oraisa. Jerusalem: Yeshivas Toras Moshe, 1989.

Oparin, A. I., ed. Origin of Life. Tokyo: Japan Scientific Societies Press, 1978.

Pagels, Heinz R. Perfect Symmetry: The Search for the Beginning of Time. New York: Simon and Schuster, 1985.

Parkes, Henry Bamford. Gods and Men: The Origins of Western Culture. New York: Alfred A. Knopf, 1959.

Prager, Dennis, and Joseph Telushkin. The Nine Questions People Ask About Judaism. New York: Simon and Schuster, 1981.

Raup, David M. "Conflicts Between Darwin and Paleontology." Bulletin (Field Museum of Natural History) 50 (January 1979).

Sachar, Abram. A History of the Jews. New York: Knopf Publishers, 1969.

Scherman, Rabbi Nosson, ed. The Complete Artscroll Siddur. New York: Mesorah Publications, Ltd., 1984.

Shapiro, Robert. Origins. New York: Summit Books, 1986.

Shirer, William Lawrence. The Rise and Fall of the Third Reich. Greenwich: Fawcett, 1950.

Stahl, Barbara J. Vertebrate History: Problems in Evolution. New York: McGraw-Hill Co., 1974.

Tillyard, Robin John. The Biology of Dragonflies. Cambridge: Cambridge University Press, 1917.

Trefil, James S. The Moment of Creation. New York: Macmillan Publishing Co., 1983.

Twain, Mark. The Complete Works of Mark Twain. American Artists Edition. New York: Harper and Brothers, 1899.

Varghese, Roy A., ed. Intellectuals Speak Out About God. Chicago:

Regnery Gateway Inc., 1984.

Velikovsky, Immanuel. *Ages in Chaos.* Vol. I. New York: Doubleday and Co., 1952.

Wardlaw, Claude Wilson. *Organization and Evolution in Plants.* London: Longmans, Green and Co., Ltd., 1965.

Zee, Anthony. *Fearful Symmetry: The Search for Beauty in Modern Physics.* New York: Macmillan Publishing Co., 1986.